THE HEART OF THE MATTER

Systemic Thinking and Practice Series

Charlotte Burck and Gwyn Daniel (Series Editors)

This influential series was co-founded in 1989 by series editors David Campbell and Ros Draper to promote innovative applications of systemic theory to psychotherapy, teaching, supervision, and organisational consultation. In 2011, Charlotte Burck and Gwyn Daniel became series editors, and aim to present new theoretical developments and pioneering practice, to make links with other theoretical approaches, and to promote the relevance of systemic theory to contemporary social and psychological questions.

Other titles in the Series include
(For a full listing, see our website www.karnacbooks.com)

The Dialogical Therapist: Dialogue in Systemic Practice
  Paolo Bertrando
Systems and Psychoanalysis: Contemporary Integrations in Family Therapy
  Carmel Flaskas and David Pocock
Intimate Warfare: Regarding the Fragility of Family Relations
  Martine Groen and Justine Van Lawick
Being with Older People: A Systemic Approach
  Edited by Glenda Fredman, Eleanor Anderson, and Joshua Stott
Mirrors and Reflections: Processes of Systemic Supervision
  Edited by Charlotte Burck and Gwyn Daniel
Race and Culture: Tools, Techniques and Trainings: A Manual for Professionals
  Reenee Singh and Sumita Dutta
The Vibrant Relationship: A Handbook for Couples and Therapists
  Kirsten Seidenfaden and Piet Draiby
The Vibrant Family: A Handbook for Parents and Professionals
  Kirsten Seidenfaden, Piet Draiby, Susanne Søborg Christensen, and
  Vibeke Hejgaard
Culture and Reflexivity in Systemic Psychotherapy: Mutual Perspectives
  Edited by Inga-Britt Krause
*Positions and Polarities in Contemporary Systemic Practice: The Legacy of
David Campbell*
  Edited by Charlotte Burck, Sara Barratt, and Ellie Kavner
Creative Positions in Adult Mental Health: Outside In–Inside Out
  Edited by Sue McNab and Karen Partridge
Emotions and the Therapist: A Systemic–Dialogical Approach
  Paolo Bertrando
*Surviving and Thriving in Care and Beyond: Personal and Professional
Perspectives*
  Sara Barratt and Wendy Lobatto
*Creativity in Times of Constraint: A Practitioner's Companion in Mental
Health and Social Care*
  Jim Wilson

THE HEART OF THE MATTER

Music and Art in Family Therapy

Hilary Palmer

Routledge
Taylor & Francis Group

LONDON AND NEW YORK

First published 2018
by Routledge
2 Park Square, Milton Park, Abingdon, Oxon OX14 4RN

and by Routledge
711 Third Avenue, New York, NY 10017

Routledge is an imprint of the Taylor & Francis Group, an informa business

British Library Cataloguing-in-Publication Data
A catalogue record for this book is available from the British Library

Library of Congress Cataloging-in-Publication Data
A catalog record has been requested for this book

ISBN: 9-781-78220-493-0 (pbk)

Typeset in Palatino
by The Studio Publishing Services Ltd
email: studio@publishingservicesuk.co.uk

CONTENTS

ACKNOWLEDGEMENTS   vii

ABOUT THE AUTHOR   xi

SERIES EDITORS' FOREWORD   xiii

FOREWORD   xv
  Peter Fraenkel

PREFACE   xix

INTRODUCTION: xxiii

CHAPTER ONE
Beginnings: a musical journey with Alice Brown   1

CHAPTER TWO
Foundations: culture and creativity   13

CHAPTER THREE
Professional contexts: music and art therapy   23

CHAPTER FOUR
A shared humanity: music, words, and the mind   37

CHAPTER FIVE
Trying something new: thoughts from the starting line   45

CHAPTER SIX
Introduction to systemic music and art techniques   53

CHAPTER SEVEN
Systemic music techniques   57

CHAPTER EIGHT
Systemic art techniques   69

CHAPTER NINE
Testing the waters: applying new methods   85

CHAPTER TEN
New horizons: implications for practice   95

CONCLUSION   111

REFERENCES   117

INDEX   127

ACKNOWLEDGEMENTS

Working with a family in therapy is a profound process involving trust, courage, curiosity, imagination, and hope from therapist and family alike. I would like to thank the families I have worked with for opening their hearts to creative ways of relating using music and art. It is through this shared experience with you that it felt important to me to write this.

This book stems from research. I found meeting with family therapists who took the plunge to become research participants an extraordinary process of learning, laughing, reflecting, and being creative with colleagues to a level I had not experienced before. You, the participants, made the research behind this publication possible. Thank you for your time, commitment, and openness to new ideas. It was great fun working with you all as co-researchers, and my thinking has developed so much from your reflections and ideas.

I would like to thank Jeremy Woodcock, the former Director of Family Therapy at the University of Bristol, where I completed my family therapy training in 2003. Jeremy's enthusiasm for my music therapy background and his excitement at the difference music could bring to family therapy encouraged me to explore and develop these ideas throughout my career, culminating in this book. Jeremy helped me believe that to be truly systemic is to allow space for the conscious and unconscious, what can be said and what cannot be said, which fitted so well with my music therapy background, allowing me to blend different ways of practising. Many thanks also go to the music therapist Hilary Wainer and art therapist Lesley Hanney for meeting with me in the very early days of my research to help hone my ideas. It was with great serendipity that I contacted the Australian music therapist Joanne McIntyre, believing her to be a long-lost school friend. Joanne has become a friend from across the seas, and helped me to keep updated on current music therapy literature.

My doctorate colleagues, Shadi Shahnavaz and Galit Haviv-Thomas, made the journey of researching this book such fun with their wonderful humour, great support, and dear friendship. It was a joy to study with them and I am very grateful for all their insightful reflections that have helped formulate my ideas, along with their great enthusiasm.

I am indebted to Charlotte Burck, who supervised my research and has championed this book. Charlotte's rigour and imagination have been invaluable and her warmth, humour, and support will always be remembered. Thank you, Charlotte, for your time, kindness, and wonderful spirit. I am very grateful to Gwyn Daniel too, series editor with Charlotte, for her encouragement. Gwyn has helped to give this book form and has gently steered me in the right direction. I also extend my thanks to Peter Fraenkel, who provided wonderful supervision from across the Atlantic, offering a musical and academic ear with great enthusiasm, humour, encouragement, and meticulous feedback.

More recently, I have found a beautiful new friend in the artist Catherine Ducker. I was deeply moved the first time I saw Catherine's work and discussed her art with her. I am very grateful to be using her painting entitled "When Colours Sing" for the cover of this book. It is a painting that, to me, encapsulates hopefulness.

I want to thank Alyson Carter, my first music therapy supervisor many years ago, for generously sharing her wisdom, creative spirit, and heart, which has led me to explore new paths and ways of thinking in all areas of my life and created a life-long bond between us. I want to thank Tim for supporting me through my doctorate, which is the basis of this book, and to Martin for kindly reading early drafts. To my other friends, who walk by my side through life's ups and downs, I want to thank you for all your invaluable love and support. You all know who you are. I also want to thank my mother, Carol, who is always cheering me on from the sidelines, and whose model of working hard to achieve positive difference in life I try to follow. You are an inspiration.

For my two beautiful girls, Hattie and Floss, I want to dance around the room shouting a huge thank you to you for your fun and funniness, your great patience and understanding, and for being proud of me. I want to thank you for playing music and dancing while I worked and for being guinea pigs to my ideas with such curiosity and willingness. You have filled the house with singing, made great suggestions, and have always kept me on my creative toes. As your mother, I will not always get it right, but I hope we can always find a way, with or without words, to connect and tell our story.

ABOUT THE AUTHOR

Hilary Palmer is a consultant family and systemic psychotherapist and qualified music therapist, working for the National Health Service (NHS) and in private practice in Surrey and Berkshire. Formerly a clinical lead in Child and Adolescent Mental Health Services (CAMHS), Hilary has worked across age ranges and began her career in the field of learning disability.

Hilary completed her doctorate at the Tavistock, London, in 2014, researching the use of music and art for families receiving a service from CAMHS. The doctorate was a culmination of a career-long interest in developing ideas and techniques that incorporate music and art in talking therapies. Hilary is currently a supervisor and tutor on the Integrated Professional Doctorate course at the Tavistock.

SERIES EDITORS' FOREWORD

Charlotte Burck and Gwyn Daniel

As family therapists we have long been committed to embracing innovation and creativity in our work and to developing innovative collaborative practices. Like other professionals, we find it difficult at times not to be constrained by our own and our institutions' habitual patterns of practice. As the drastic cuts to services, driven by the government's austerity programme, have been implemented, professionals in the public sector have been called on to work harder in less time and with increasingly complex and challenging situations. In this context, practitioners can become risk averse and less likely to expand their own creative potential and that of the families we meet. It is therefore a complete joy to have Hilary Palmer's book to enable us to put the heart of creativity back in the matter, and to have her persuasive account of how it really does make a difference. Hilary Palmer has always woven music into her work with families as well as into her own living. What makes this book such a significant contribution to the field is that she has set out to explore with other family therapists how they too could enhance their practice through the use of music and art. Through these joint explorations Hilary and her colleagues have developed many further creative possibilities for incorporating music and art into the child and adolescent mental health services in which they are based.

The book is full of riches. Hilary traces the importance of music and art within different cultures, a question of theoretical interest but that can also be helpfully raised in meetings with families themselves. She provides many exercises for practitioners and gives moving examples of work with families, both from her own work and that of the collaborating clinicians. Here are powerful examples of how significant communications within families and within therapy happen outside words, to supplement and complement our habitual concentration on verbal interactions, and how playfulness can in fact tap into serious matters.

Having invited other therapists to develop these ways of working with individuals and families alongside her, Hilary Palmer became ever more curious about how change is enabled for therapists themselves and the organisations within which they work. As readers we are invited to reflect on our relationships to music and art and other ways of being creative, and to consider how we could draw on these and families' own creativities together. Beliefs about therapist identities became highlighted as a possible constraint, as training courses have mainly neglected to incorporate these components of clinical work. Persuading ourselves that music and art tap into the "heart of the matter" and that we are prepared to risk ourselves in making use of them is therefore a major hurdle. By including the conversations between Hilary and her collaborators in which they provide feedback on their mutual endeavours, we are invited into a vivid narrative of the joys, the challenges, and the constraints of introducing new, creative, and playful dimensions into their work. Their conversations and reflections stimulate our own ideas about how to develop these in our practice. They also invite us to think about how we can make spaces and opportunities for such enhancements in our own organisations.

We are delighted to have Hilary Palmer's book in our series. We cannot but imagine that you will take up her invitation and find ways to develop a new or renewed relationship to music, art, and creativity for yourselves and for your practice.

FOREWORD

Peter Fraenkel

When family therapy first emerged in the 1950s, it was in part as a reaction against the perceived limitations of the reigning psychoanalytic paradigm. Many of family therapy's creators—Don Jackson, Murray Bowen, Carl Whittaker, Lyman Wynne, and Salvador Minuchin—were psychiatrists and psychoanalytically trained, and they felt constrained by many aspects of this approach. Other pioneers—such as Gregory Bateson, Jay Haley, Paul Watzlawick, and Virginia Satir—came to their interest in families by way of anthropology, communication theory, and humanistic, experiential psychology —all focused more on action than on words. One of those perceived limitations was that psychoanalytic psychotherapy focused largely on the patient's verbalisations, to the relative neglect of their non-verbal interactional behaviour. As a result, the first few decades of family therapy focused largely on interactions among family members, privileging attention to process over content. Minuchin was known to tell trainees (like myself) that he was always grateful when the topics couples and families presented as the content of their conflicts were relatively trivial—differences in loading a washing machine (whether to put the soap in last or first), whether to put a child to bed at 8.00 p.m. *vs.* 8.30 p.m., how warm or cool to keep the ambient temperature of their home, and the endless variations of fights about finances. He attuned us to the repetitive interactional processes underlying these content discussions, and that typically replicated across content domains. Therapy focused on changing these patterns, not on talking about thoughts and feelings about the surface problem per se. Changes in relational patterning, which is what he meant by "family structure", led to changes in thoughts and feelings, not, as psycho-analysis held, the other way around. Family therapy held that insight was not required for behaviour change; if anything, changes in behaviour might lead to new perspectives and understanding. The key to a successful session was to introduce novelty right there in the moment, to provide a place for new experiencing, a goal that the great Virginia Satir also emphasised, through different, more emotion-based means.

But starting in the early 1980s, with the introduction of post-modernism, the field of family therapy started to shift back to conversations about thoughts, and sometimes feelings, and away from observation of, and intervention upon, here-and-now interaction. Because reality was viewed as socially constructed—and constructed primary through linguistically-mediated meanings—therapists now asked family members, each in turn, how they thought about themselves and their problems. Therapists started to shy away from commenting on what they observed in those discussions, in part because another premise of postmodernism was that reality is relative, particular, and "idiographic" to each family, not based on universal principles observed, with important variations, across families and cultures. As a result, therapists could no longer accurately and even ethically hold the position of "expert observer", assessing patterns viewed as problematic, based on nomothetic clinical theory and research about how families are organised and function. The emphasis became helping family members locate their own images of healthy relationships, their nascent solutions, restoring subordinated narratives of strength and coping, rather than the therapist directly guiding them into unimaginable new ways of being with one another. Whereas the original metaphors in family therapy were of the "couple's dance", and achieving "harmony"; whereas therapists used to get members up on their feet to demonstrate problems and desired outcomes through Peggy Papp's playful technique of "family sculpting"; and several drawings hung on institute walls of Minchin as a conductor of a "family orchestra", the advent of narrative and other postmodern/

poststructuralist therapies substituted a linguistic metaphor, the "family's narrative".

To many of us lucky enough to be trained by the early masters, this is a loss, a return to what I have called "the hegemony of words". For sure, the postmodern, linguistic approaches have added an important corrective to an over-focus solely on behaviour and in-the-moment emotional expression, and we have become importantly more collaborative in our work with families, valuing their expertise on their own lives. But with our increasing grasp of the neuroscience behind intimate relationships, postmodern, language-based approaches have inadvertently directed us to access mostly the left hemisphere and higher cortical regions, to the neglect of other parts of the brain and associated experience: sub cortical structures like cochlear nuclei, the brain stem, and the cerebellum, the auditory cortices on both sides of the brain, lower parts of the frontal lobes, the visual cortex, the motor and sensory cortex, and the temporal lobes, especially the amygdala— so central to the modulation of emotion—all of which are involved when we listen to and produce music, and when we create visual art, or dance. As Daniel Levitin has shown us in his brilliant book, *This is Your Brain on Music* (2006), listening to and playing music is a truly "whole brain" activity. The same goes for other artistic expressions.

Enter Hilary Palmer and this outstanding, innovative book. Hilary brings a long career as a singer and musician to her work as a therapist, training first to be a music therapist, and then a family therapist. Through a brilliant review of the role of music and art in the cultures within which families are embedded, and through her in-depth qualitative research on the impact of training colleagues to introduce music and art into therapy, she makes a powerful case to expand the range of our therapeutic practices to incorporate these artistic modalities. Powerful case material peppers this book, showing how music and art can result in enhanced self-expression and new, healing interactions among family members. Hilary's approach is integrative, a "both-and", rather than an "either" (language) "or" (music and art): the families she describes play music and make art together, and talk about the experience of new and renewed connection, which leads to more music and art, in a lovely positive spiral of change full of surprise, tears, humour, and joy. She helps us rediscover that meaning does not only exist in words; there is "meaning in motion", as we play together with sounds, objects, and images. This is a groundbreaking book, one that I highly recommend to all therapists, and it should have a central place in family therapy training programmes, and in the clinics and practices of all family therapists. Her work provides us a path to guide families towards "the heart of the matter". To quote the great American soul singer Barry White, "Let the music play!"

PREFACE

"... he paints his pictures in sounds; he makes the very silences speak; he expresses his ideas as feelings and his feelings as accents and the passions that he voices move us to the very depths of our hearts"

(Jean-Jacques Rousseau, cited in Day & Le Huray, 1988)

Finding the "heart of the matter" is about discovering the human core around which interactions and actions revolve. But what is the heart? I give you my heart, you are my sweetheart, it was heartfelt, all point to something more than, something "other", something beyond words, caught in an action, an expression, or in a feeling. If therapy is about creating an alliance to discover the heart of the matter, and resolve conflicts that might stand in the way of people reaching their potential to live a fulfilled life, then the means by which we get to that heart need to be explored. When working with families, it means discovering the collective heart of the matter that might involve myriad different ideas, feelings, and narratives that can somehow sit side by side. I could say that it was my heart that led me to become a therapist, a tug or a pull that I wanted to work with young people and their families. I love my work because it touches my heart and allows me heart to heart contact with others.

As a newly qualified music therapist twenty years ago, I remember the first time I invited a parent to join a child's individual session. I took the child into the music room, and, as I walked in, I realised the child primarily needed to be interacting with her mother, not with me. I turned straight around and invited the mother to join us. What followed was a profound interactive process in which a mother and a child, who had become increasingly isolated from each other due to the child's deteriorating condition, found a way to communicate, to be in dialogue, and to express themselves through the media of music. From then on, whenever possible, I invited families to join their children in the musical space. Curious about expanding my knowledge in work with families, I trained as a family therapist and have continued combining music therapy and systemic ideas ever since.

The writing of this book is led by a love of the arts and the witnessing of how useful music and art can be in facilitating positive change for families. Curious about whether music and art were being used by other family therapists in the field, I conducted some action research. I was very aware of my ease in using music, given my background as a musician and music therapist, and keen to think with colleagues about whether there were simple transferable skills that could be taught and might be useful for therapists of all backgrounds to use in their work with families—both those who describe themselves as musical and those who view themselves as non-musical.

It was also important to include art because, for many practitioners, it is a more readily available medium, providing a rich resource of creative possibilities that vastly expand the repertoire of options when working non-verbally. I have worked with art therapy colleagues, have experienced art therapy myself from the client position, and have a personal understanding that art offers a unique way of expressing ideas, thoughts, and emotions that can lead to gaining insight. In my experience of art therapy as a client, my paintings allowed me to express aspects of myself that I did not fully understand and that had not yet found a way to be verbally explored or communicated. The process came in touch with the heart of the matter in a way that my brain and use of words might have censored, edited, and processed in accordance with the known self, therefore not allowing the unknown self to be explored as fully as possible. I have yet to walk into a family therapy room where there has not been pens and paper at the disposal of therapist and client alike. Yet, although all this equipment is an acknowledgement that, at the very least, many children like to draw, the talking therapists' use of art medium with families has never been fully explored. Family therapists readily use genograms, and might encourage children to draw a picture of their family or feelings, perhaps to externalise a problem, but our scope in terms of using this readily accessible non-verbal medium appears limited. I once heard that the talking therapist's "art" was the art of asking questions. I was curious to ask whether, if we reflect on what we do, art itself may be able to play a useful role, too.

For Hattie and Floss

Introduction

This book invites you to consider the use of music and art in your work with families. It introduces systemic techniques using music and art, giving a rationale for their use, and providing feedback from practitioners who have explored and incorporated the techniques in their work. I consider what it is to try something new, the personal challenges faced, and the implications for our professional identity. Against a backdrop of exploration into what creativity is, the history of the arts in therapy, and consideration of what happens when we use words, I present a case for music and art to be incorporated as an adjunct to our practice with families.

Music and art are very different media. While having much in common, as both are non-verbal and evoke feeling states, the differences in the experience of producing music and art offer the practitioner a vast palette of ideas and opportunities. These can be dipped into depending on the practitioners' own sensibilities and the needs and personalities of the families they work with. Art is tangible and, through colour, depth, and perspective, our sense of sight is called upon for us to engage emotionally and experience the image, sculpture, or objects in front of us. For the therapist and family, it leaves a visual record of a process undertaken that can be returned to and changed, expanded, or reviewed. Music is transient; we are called upon to hear, feel, and often physically move in response. Music demands us to be present in the moment and offers opportunities for relating with immediacy and feeling. For therapists, music and art both offer the possibility of interacting without words as part of the therapeutic process.

Using music and art in family therapy is not about a finished product, although that can have its place, it is about engagement in a non-verbal process with others that allows families to be present in the moment, communicate on a level playing field, activate different neurological responses, and experience a predominantly feeling, rather than thinking, self in relation to others. Family therapy theory and practice has not, in the past, set a huge store by people being able to express their feelings more freely. This book argues the case that to reach the heart of the matter, opportunities to experience being with each other in the here and now in a creative way, and to express feelings without the risks inherent in using words, can be an invaluable adjunct to our work.

I am dual trained in music therapy and family and systemic psychotherapy. Throughout the book, I speak of family therapy and family therapists. However, this book is written to be accessible to any therapist that works with families, of any discipline and training, so please feel welcomed and included whatever your background.

The subject of using live art making in family therapy has received some attention in the family therapy field (Carlson, 1997; Colahan & Robinson, 2002; Kerr & Hoshino, 2008; Lowenstein, 2010; Rober, 2009). As for using music, there are some references to the use of pre-recorded music in family therapy literature (Hendricks & Bradley, 2005; Mang Keung Ho & Settles, 1984) but literature on live music making in sessions is limited (Palmer, 2002).

In the art therapy and music therapy professions, the focus, until recently, has been on individual and group work that is rooted in psychodynamic theory. However, systemic ideas have a long history of being considered in the art therapy profession (Kwiatkowska, 1978; Riley, 2000; Shafer, 2008) and are receiving growing attention in music therapy (Cobbett, 2016; McIntyre, 2009; Nemesh, 2017a,b).

The techniques presented in this book are the result of an action research project that involved working with three teams of family therapists, in three different NHS Trusts, all working in child and adolescent mental health. The participant therapists became co-researchers, and the techniques presented in this book are the products of experimenting and playing with the initial music and art ideas I introduced to the teams. Therefore, what you have here is the harvest from a crop tended by many, to feed you and encourage further crop planting.

The book begins with a case study. In the case study, I am a family therapy trainee using music in a family therapy setting for the first time. The case study highlights the rationale for this book, highlighting the potential benefit of using non-verbal media, considering the wider constraints, and thinking about how we engage clients and create something meaningful for them. Music and art are so culturally positioned that a discussion on culture and creativity and what it means to be delivering and receiving music and art seemed necessary. Similarly, it was important to pay homage to the music therapy and art therapy professions through considering the rich history of working with music and art therapeutically in a chapter that considers both music and art therapy, and the history of these art forms in family therapy. I believe music and art can help to create mindful spaces and this is explored in the context of brain function and language to argue the case for music and art to be considered due to their influence on multiple levels of human functioning. From these foundations, the techniques are introduced, and who better to do this than the family therapists who participated in my research and took these ideas forward. You will hear their voices as they celebrated, struggled, became inspired by, and questioned the place of music and art in their practice. Implementing something different and new is fraught with myriad personal and professional quandaries, dilemmas, and risks. I hope that through their experiences, your own feelings can be validated, and that through their spirit of adventure, you will be inspired. All the techniques include a rationale for use and, where possible, feedback from practitioners who have used the techniques is included, as well as case studies from my own practice.

Fraenkel (2013) states that "the key to successful therapy is that it captures the imagination of our clients", and that "there is much outside our practice we need to access . . . to formulate our interventions". This book hopes to help us capture the imagination of our clients through igniting our creativity to use music and art in our work. Just as we ask families to venture out of their comfort zones when engaging in therapy, often far more than we can possibly imagine, this book invites you to do the same. As a reader, I would like you to take a position of curiosity and continue the exploration and development of the ideas presented in this book. See the techniques as a list of ingredients and instructions to add your own flavours, expertise, and flair to, in search of a fit for you culturally, personally and professionally. Most importantly, have fun and play!

CHAPTER ONE

Beginnings: a musical journey with Alice Brown

During the early years of my family and systemic psychotherapy training, I had an honorary contract on an adolescent unit where I first began thinking about transferable skills and ideas between the arts therapy professions and systemic practice. Let me introduce you to Alice and our journey together as a way of illustrating how this book began. The chapter concludes with an exploration of how being dual trained has affected my position and identity as a therapist.

Meeting up with Alice again

I had worked at the adolescent inpatient unit before, as a music therapist, mainly doing group work. When this work ceased after two years, I had already begun my family therapy training and requested to remain on the unit in an honorary capacity, as part of their family therapy team. It was in this role that I met Alice again. Alice was fifteen years old and from a white, middle-class background. She had experienced several inpatient admissions over a three-year period due to depression and deliberate self-harm. Alice had received individual psychology and art therapy in the past; the latter she had particularly enjoyed and found useful.

Alice had attended my music therapy group over a three-term period a year previously; she was pleased to see me and bemoaned the fact that I had stopped working as a music therapist on the unit. The family had been working in family therapy for some time and, throughout this period, had requested for Alice to meet with each parent separately, rather than as a whole family group, as they felt this would be too overwhelming for all concerned. Mr Brown felt that Alice had exhausted talking about things and so the family were offered the opportunity for me to join the two therapists working directly with the family in the room, to offer some music into the sessions. Alice was excited about this prospect and felt she might be able to work with both her mother and father together if music was used.

Alice and her family attended four sessions where music was used over a six-month period. These sessions were alternated with talking only sessions. The team consisted of two family therapists, two specialist registrar doctors who were on rotation, and who acted as a reflecting team, and me. Below is a brief description of the content of each session, followed by reflections from the team about the work. These were gathered from retrospective interviews held three months after the last session.

Session one

The family was asked to choose instruments for each other which represented each of them. Mr Brown was given the ocean drum as he was constantly on the move and liked things to be harmonious. Alice also felt he should have the cymbal because sometimes he would flare up in anger. Alice was given the djembe drum by her mother because Alice had quickly stated that it was her favourite. Her mother explained that it looked as if it had great scope to make a variety of sounds, and had a depth and darkness. Alice responded that it was good because you could "communicate whatever the feeling". Mrs Brown was given the xylophone to symbolise someone quiet but complex. Alice then chose instruments for the two therapists and me.

With the instruments chosen, I introduced the idea of improvisation. After a period of silence, Alice began to play her drum, it was tentative to begin with but careful and steady. Gradually, family members and the team joined in. At the end of the music, Alice asked why I had not played the handbell which was beside me and had instead played a small drum only. I explained that I was concerned about making too much impact and the music being all about me. Mrs Brown shared this view and said she wanted to play the high notes on her xylophone but was worried about speaking out and being "out of sync". Alice responded to her mother, saying that she should have played what she felt because Alice would have made it "in sync". It was noted that Mr Brown had not used the cymbal—he had not become angry.

The family was then asked whether they would like to continue to improvise or would like to create a sculpt using the instruments they had chosen for one another (see the chapter on music techniques for ideas on how to do this). They opted for a sculpt and chose further instruments for absent family members. Mr Brown was chosen by the family to lead the sculpt. During the sculpt, Alice was able to express that she needed "something emotionally". Alice left the session saying that she felt "confident and experimental". Mr Brown felt the session had helped to represent things that were hard to put into words and, at the end of the session, he spoke of feeling that they were nearly at the crux of the matter when it was time to stop.

Session two

On arrival at the unit, I realised that I had forgotten to bring my instruments. I felt quite silly and suggested the session be a talking one instead. However, the two therapists were keen not to disappoint the family and for it to be a music session. We scavenged around the unit for instruments and came up with a motley collection of half broken, homemade, and toy instruments. I felt rather foolish and disappointed with myself. I also felt quite vulnerable without the beautiful professional percussion instruments I usually had with me. However, I was encouraged by the therapists' enthusiasm and resourcefulness.

Alice arrived at the session with her father only and, although somewhat disappointed, she also appeared amused that I had forgotten my instruments and laughed at the strange collection we had pooled together. We tried to improvise, but we all felt rather held back by the limited tonal quality of the instruments. However, Alice was keen to keep trying. Mr Brown spoke about how it was typical for Alice to make positive things happen from nothing; he felt Alice to be a "go getter", but also cut off, and thought the music sessions revealed this. In return, Alice expressed that the music revealed this because the music sessions were more helpful than the talking ones.

The session ended with Alice suggesting that we play an improvisation about a person. She chose Maria, the art therapist on the unit, whom she had worked with previously. Alice chose instruments and led the music with a plastic Fisher Price apple, which had a lovely, Tibetan-sounding bell inside. The sound of the bell was quite resonant in comparison to the other instruments and Alice thought it symbolised Maria well. The improvisation felt like a coming together and Alice appeared very satisfied with the result.

Session three

The family came to the session in good spirits. "Things" had been going well since we last met. Continuing the theme of the last session, Alice suggested that she would like everyone to improvise about each member of the family while the person chosen sat and listened. This took up the whole session and resulted in intermittent and avid discussions around issues of trying and not getting it quite right, levels of understanding, and knowing and not knowing each other.

Session four

Alice had mixed feelings about attending this last session, she had a headache and she and her mum had just had a "blow out". Alice explained that she felt frustrated when she could not make people understand and went from being angry to being scared. I asked Alice if we could help her put some of these feelings into music to help us understand better, and if she could choose instruments for us and lead an improvisation about being scared. Before we commenced, we set out some clear boundaries for the music to keep it safe. These included a clear decision that the music would rise up and then die away slowly, thereby making sure that the music was contained in a frame-work which would allow Alice's experience to be both supported and held by her family and the therapists, and not become out of control and overwhelming.

The improvisation was powerful and Alice felt that it went some way to being able to express her feelings; she also felt that these feelings had been heard by her parents. Where the music had not expressed her feelings adequately, Alice was able to begin to put into words what it felt like to be scared. After the music finished, Alice was able to move on from her angry/scared feelings and share that she felt, in general, her relationship with her mother was improving. She spoke of casual moments they had shared which made her feel more connected. We reviewed how the family had felt using music over the last six months and whether it had been helpful. Mr and Mrs Brown felt that everyone had been there "trying to understand and make sense of things" and the music had helped this to happen. Alice stated, "I wanted it to help us talk about things and it certainly did that."

Responses from the team and wider setting

I interviewed the two family therapists working with the family sepa-rately, three months after the last session. Unfortunately, the two doctors who acted as a reflecting team had left the unit and were, therefore, unavailable to be interviewed.

The team's hopes and expectations of the work were that the family would find a way to express different emotions, and that the music might help them find the words they needed to express these emotions verbally. They felt that the family had struggled in family therapy but that the talking had become easier since the music sessions commenced. Both therapists had talked about the work with colleagues on the unit. These conversations were mainly to nursing staff and other therapists who felt that the use of music might help the family think in a more abstract way. Nursing colleagues were inter-ested and thought the approach was new and unusual. The manager–clinical nurse specialist also supported the work. It is interesting that one of the therapists specifically avoided conversing with the consul-tant psychiatrist about the work, as he felt that the psychiatrist might not understand what the team was trying to achieve. The therapist was concerned that the approach might not be valued and not be taken seriously. The work was also mentioned in a positive way to the community team in the locality to which Alice was being discharged.

The team felt that the music became a metaphor in their work with Alice and brought out the emotional styles of family members. In this way, they felt the family discovered a unique way to be together and think about feelings in a safe space. One therapist said he experienced honesty in the work and felt it was very empowering for Alice, especially as she had experienced music therapy before and could bring her knowledge and experiences into the work with her parents. The therapists commented that they witnessed the family "free up". In previous "talking only" sessions, Alice and her mother had worried that anything they said might exacerbate their problems, whereas the team perceived that music allowed them to relax and communicate in a non-threatening way.

When asked whether the talking only sessions with the family had changed at all since the music sessions began, the male therapist commented that the atmosphere was "palpably less tense" and that the therapist found himself being less annoyed and challenging to the family and had instead adopted a more narrative approach. He felt the music sessions had helped Alice co-construct a new image for herself from the one usually seen by Alice's parents. The female therapist spoke of overcoming a boundary because "somehow we had all been through the experience [of playing music] together" and this helped engagement.

It was felt that the use of music had created a space for doing something differently and for the team it had felt liberating, although one of the therapists expressed that she had worried that the music element might constrain her from doing her best because she was not musical. While welcoming the opening up of boundaries, there was also some concern that because the music did not fit in with the traditional view of family therapy, there was a danger that it would not be taken seriously.

The therapists felt that the work had reinforced the idea for them that action ways of working can be good to use, especially with young people who found it hard to engage in talking therapies. Neither therapist felt confident to use the methods of working I had engaged the family in on their own, but felt that the work had generally affected how they engage with families and gain trust.

The team's lasting impressions of the work were that it made tense and uncomfortable work more bearable. It was felt that Mrs Brown had been at her most committed in the music sessions and able/willing to change her position and construct new meanings. The therapists felt the work had challenged the whole team and heightened the idea of multiple perspectives. It was suggested that, just as Anderson and Goolishan (1988) stress the importance of meaning through words, meaning could also be created and expressed through music, and that it was a different, but equally important, way for voices to be heard.

Reflections

In music therapy, the therapist is an integral part of the music making. This was quite new for the team and appeared to help us meet the family on an equal footing and share new experiences. One of the family therapists described themselves as musical and one as not musical. Of particular help to the family was having a non-musical member of the team participating, as this added an element of moral support and mutual discovery. Through looking at strengths within musical interactions and exploring differences, new discourses arose for the team, as well as for the family, which allowed a move away from the dominant discourse of fragility and stuck-ness that surrounded the work. Within the improvised music, musical conversations developed that allowed the family and team to interact in a fun and non-confrontational way. This helped to explore how the beliefs, actions, and feelings of the family were interconnected and meanings created.

In keeping with the view that a different way of seeing things is essential for change, I was conscious that the experiences gained through the music process helped the family to begin to reframe themselves and interrupt the problem-saturated cycle. Choosing instruments for each other allowed for insight to individual lenses and an exploration of the family members' perception of each other. This technique also explored how we want to be seen and how we think we are seen by others. The improvisations themselves took on a narrative flavour and each musical improvisation could be described as a "mutually validating conversation" (Dallos & Draper, 2000). In many ways, the sculpt did not differ from any other sculpt in a family therapy setting; it just used musical instruments instead of people or objects. However, there was always the opportunity available that, when the instruments were in place, each person could be given a voice by the playing of various instruments in various combinations, allowing for themes to be explored further and absent family members to be actively included.

I was very encouraged by the work, but disappointed that the team felt they would not attempt anything similar in my absence. My experience as a music therapist put me in an expert position and I was left to consider how I could have made the experience more collaborative and enhanced the accessibility of music as a medium for the talking therapists to use. Alice was also very much a customer for the use of music; she had a positive experience in music therapy previously and a good therapeutic relationship with me.

Thinking about Alice and ideas about change

As I progressed through my family therapy training and into the role of family therapist, my professional identity and working practice developed through a coming together of different theoretical stances. As a result, I have a theoretical identity that is systemic, but inclusive of psychodynamic theory, and it is in this context that I practise.

In systemic terms, the individual is seen in the context of the intimate connections of which she or he is currently a part (Gorell Barnes, 1998), the social constructions, and dominant and subjugated narratives within that person's family and culture. I believe that there is "continual change through exchange" (Hoffman, 1995) and that some of these realities are discovered through social discourse (Real, 1990). However, in the context of my work with Alice, I was also interested to discover through what other "exchanges" involving art and music, new realities can emerge.

My theory of change is influenced by psychodynamic thinking, in which resistance to change can be seen as the product of unresolved conflict on an individual's developmental pathway. However, as a relationally thinking family therapist, I have married this with Stern's (1985) concept of "self" in which the development of self and relationships are two sides of the same issue, with a belief that development is a process in which self and relationships are co-dependent. For Alice, it was in the repairing of fractures in her relationship with her parents that allowed her to develop a deeper sense of herself.

I am also influenced by attachment theory in thinking about the connections between past and present relational experiences, and how this influences both the ability to change and what that change will look like. I wonder if the music in some sense allowed Alice to revisit an earlier developmental stage when relating to her parents was fun and easy, and the use of music allowed for a relived experience which acted as a bridge to the here and now.

I believe the process of change is a complex web of interaction often broken and remade until it fits with each family. Therefore, in thinking about creating difference we must honour a client's theory of change. Alice knew that she wanted to use music. She had experienced a music therapy group and it had helped, and she had found art therapy helpful. Therefore, Alice came to the experience with the knowledge that working in a non-verbal way can create positive difference. Mason (1993) believes that there needs to be a sense of not knowing and an openness to learn about how individual systems work. In our not knowing, or "safe uncertainty", I believe the therapist is liberated to discover her unique relationship to change within each family system she works with. The therapists working with Alice embraced this not knowing position both through facing the challenge of using music for the first time, and being open to different concepts of what change might look like for the family and how this might be realised.

In thinking about Bateson's (1972) statement that: "too much consciousness may make impossible some desired sequence of events", Hoffman (1995, p. 44) argues that it is the therapist who should be restrained from change. Hoffman wishes to minimise the consciousness of therapist in pushing, or strategising, for change, and believes that change is facilitated in the creation of space where it can evolve unawares. Papp (1983), on the other hand, brings our attention to the rich complexities involved in changing a system in the hope of more consciously utilising those complexities in the service of producing change. I believe both positions are valuable. In music therapy, change often occurs unawares as a client could gain insight into his feelings without conscious effort, or change the way he relates to others, while unconscious of the process. Often, a musical exchange can be left in the music and not verbalised. However, there is also a music therapy stance in which music is very much used as a means to an end, in which desired change is named and is consciously worked towards. I believe Alice, her family, the team, and I experienced change on both these levels.

Change forces us into a different place, and with each change comes a grappling with ourselves over a new identity that is influenced by cultural narrative, social and family networks, and our own intrapsychic make-up and development. I believe change occurs in the intersubjective space in which people are linked through language and social actions (Hoffman, 1995), which, in turn, might trigger internal or intrapsychic changes. However, I also believe that this space contains unspoken emotional resonances and communication that, if given a voice, can assist these changes, as I believe was the case for Alice.

Carnevale (1999) uses the term "re-making" when describing the caring and comforting process of a family towards a severely ill child. I believe the term "re-making" is more systemic than the word "change". To re-make is to use familiar concepts, ideas, and experiences to create something different, but not detached, from one's previous knowledge of the world. In this way, the past and its role in creating the future is acknowledged in an analogous way to Byng Hall's concept (Hills, 2002) of "re-scripting" family experiences in which action and beliefs are connected in recursive loops. From a music therapy perspective, the music allowed Alice and her parents to experience what it was like to be once again in synchronicity with one another and use this experience to begin to re-make their relationship.

Holding with my social constructionist beliefs, I am interested in narrative therapy, which believes that fuelling actions and beliefs are those family narratives that constitute identities, lives, and problems. Problems are created by oppressive stories (dominant narratives) that do not fit with a person's lived experience. Therefore, narrative therapy opens the space to create alternative stories through a reauthoring of personal narratives. I believe music and art allow for the parts of our stories that are beyond words to find expression and be witnessed.

I believe that reauthoring does not necessarily need to focus on words for the creation of alternative ways of seeing the world or understanding experience, but can be explored through non-verbal means. Bateson (1972) called for therapists to engage both "rigour" and "imagination" in their work, believing that the artist's or poet's vision of reality was as profound as the scientist's, even though the chain of logic might not be as easy to demonstrate, or the process as wholly conscious as scientific enquiry. Bateson's views on the arts in therapy and the role of intuition were positive. Third order cybernetics embraces this creativity, allowing for a sense of play, emotionality, and imagination. It is my belief that using music and art can "enhance the families' effective freedom to change" (Tomm, 1984) to be "remade" and to "reauthor", in a child friendly context that invites playfulness and imagination. This belief is fuelled by my own experiences of transferring my knowledge from the music therapy profession to being a family therapist. The work with Alice highlighted that non-verbal means provided opportunities for difference and change in the way Alice's family communicated and interacted, which, in turn, allowed for insight to be gained and connections to be re-made.

CHAPTER TWO

Foundations: culture and creativity

T o understand any art or music, an understanding of cultural context is crucial. When using music and art in family therapy, we draw upon new levels of context and need to be aware of the complexities and riches encompassed in these contexts. Music and art are fundamental acts of humankind, and it is with this in mind that a discussion on what it is to give, receive, and be in union through music and art is fundamental to the premise of this book.

To start from the very beginning, in Palaeolithic cave paintings depicting animals, symbols, dancing, and flutes, a world where art and music is necessity, not luxury, is evidenced. The paintings on the cave wall were practical in origin, used to record, plan, communicate, and control. In the depicting of an animal, the hunter–gatherer is instilled with magical powers over the animal he has drawn, and, therefore, art becomes significant to survival itself (Storr, 1992).

Australian aborigines are believed to be the oldest culture on earth and are thought to have devoted more time to art than any other race in history. Stories, art, and paintings were used as a means to remember information, for example, where sacred sites were, as well as to indicate areas to avoid, and where food supplies could be found. Paintings and engravings were made on bark, caves, sand, didgeridoos, boomerangs, huts, possum coats, and on their bodies. However, beyond art as a practical tool, art was used to express "Dreamtime". According to aboriginal belief, all life—human, animal, bird, and fish—is part of one unchanging web of relationships that can be traced back to the beginning of time, the Dreamtime. The beginning of creation is enacted through music and dance and captured in art in an experience called "dreaming", which continues to be central to the spiritual lives of aboriginal people today.

Similarly to Aboriginal culture, aesthetic ideas and practices in Asia combine mind, body, and spirit with the material world, and are highly valued as a way to express ideas that cannot be grasped in language alone. The Japanese Buddhist priest Kukai (774–835) summed up the teachings of his Chinese master Huigo in the following words:

> The abbot informed me that the esoteric scriptures are so abstruse that their meaning cannot be conveyed except through art. For this reason, he ordered the court artist Li Chen and about a dozen other painters to execute ten scrolls of the womb and Diamond mandalas. (Tsunoda et al., 1958, p. 141)

We inhabit a culture reliant on the visual and the verbal, with the visual, more times than not, being linked to words, stereotyped imagery, and consumerism. As McGilchrist (2009) argues, it is in the West that we have lost the central position of music in society as part of communal life, unlike most other parts of the world: "relegating music to the side lines of life . . . competition and specialisation have made music something compartmentalised, somewhere from life's core" (p. 104). In the history of the world, music is not an individualistic or solitary experience. In non-Western cultures, music plays an integral part in celebration, healing, religious festivals, working life, and recreation, primarily through shared performance and not just the passive activity of listening. An example of this is the Bolivian Andes. Here, music is associated with agricultural production and each instrument and dance has a seasonal significance. Appropriate music played in the correct context brings good fortune and maintains bodily health. Illness, therefore, is linked to inappropriate contact with musical beings which can cause ill health, madness, or death. *Sirinus* (sirens) is the magical sprit that all new musical creations are attributed to. Healing, therefore, is conducted through playing music as a consolation, to appease the forces that oversee fortune in the community. In Bolivian culture, music is related to *animu* (energy) which is attributed to all living things and, as *animu* is connected to sound, movement, light, and scent, sound is equivalent to life, and its shaping in music maybe seen as the shaping of life (Stobart, 2000).

Music is also central in African culture. *Ngoma* (translated as "drum") is an ancient African ritual and therapeutic process in which music is central. *Ngoma* is about song, dance, and catharsis and involves discerning spirits within the music to induce healing. Although music in Western society is not cast as specifically healing, people are drawn to it for that purpose, and musical events can generate a sense of connection and shared participation that go beyond the construction of music as players before an audience to a similar experience to that in Africa where rhythm, bodily movement, sound, and words are a conversation that grows in intensity and fullness (Janzen, 2000). However, in Western society, music is not considered a cultural necessity and an integral part of being human; instead, it is often placed in specific contexts where it is deemed appropriate. As therapists in the West, it is this context we work in, and these barriers that need to be understood before offering difference. This is particularly the case for family therapists when using a medium that is not in the job title. If you go to a concert or exhibition, you are opting to experience art and music on some level; likewise, if seeing a music or art therapist, the description "is on the tin". Family therapists may need to embrace wider descriptions of themselves and what they do to encompass this difference, as can be seen in Chapter Five when I explore what it is to try something new.

What all the above examples have in common is music and art being used to fulfil a job, whether it is to appease spirits, grow crops, celebrate, make a political statement, document history, or convey what cannot be described in words. In this way, music and art are used as a vehicle across all cultures and contexts, some as an integral element of life, as in Bolivia, as essential to healing, as in Africa, to document and tell stories, as in native Australia, or to express emotions and political thoughts, as in the West. In the West, music is associated primarily with recreational activity that is played out in the space created between performer and audience. There is also a strong story-telling history in blues, jazz, and folk traditions. However, performing music and producing works of art are seen as something predominantly for the trained and talented, and not part of the essence of day-to-day life. There are many overlaps in the use of both music and art cross-culturally, the difference being that the importance of music and art in each culture, and the value attributed to it, varies remarkably.

In Western contemporary culture over the past fifty years, music is often seen as a luxury, an added extra, and often sidelined in education curriculum planning as optional. In an effort to address this issue, the government created a National Plan for Music Education with a specific programme to run from 2012–2015 (that has now been extended to 2020) to fund music education hubs. These hubs were created to give children the opportunity to learn an instrument in school, with opportunities also for joining a choir. Free art clubs on Saturdays for 14–16-year-olds, more school visits to museums, and specific training opportunities in dance for the gifted and talented were also created (DoE, 2011). However, in a report published on 15 November 2013, Ofsted criticised the programme for not being successful enough at improving music education in schools, reporting that only a minority of pupils were benefiting and in two-thirds of schools they visited there was little discernible difference. What this illustrates is that a deficit was found within music education in schools, and even when this was funded with a £292-million programme to create change, the change has struggled to be realised. It is in this climate that we operate as therapists and although efforts to value music within education, and, therefore, in society, are being made, the fundamental value of the arts in society remains relatively low.

However, hope can be gleaned from Western culture's relegating of music to enhance pleasure and, as Austern (2000, p. 113) expresses it: "marketed as medication for the self-cure of whatever ails body and soul, most often the pangs and fits of unrequited love" and especially for cases of "melancholy".

The history of the discussion on melancholy, which can be charted from Aristotle to twentieth-century psychiatrists such as Freud, is commonly linked throughout history with a definition focused on sorrow and depression. Melancholy is also associated with an equally strong theme of love, both the desire for spiritual union with a divine being and for the emotional and physical hunger for sexual satisfaction, often described as a "great despairing cry for love" (Austern, 2000).

In 1632, Burton wrote, "Many men are made melancholy by hearing music but it is a pleasing melancholy that it causeth, and therefore to such as our discontent . . . it expels cares . . . and easeth in an instant" (p. 297).

Despite the lack of music as an integral part of Western culture, music's clear link with expressing joy and easing the pain of melancholy over many centuries gives us a strong foundation of cultural "knowing" on which to base our therapeutic interventions. It is, therefore, important for us as family therapists to remain inquisitive about how this embedded phenomenon has been experienced already by those we work with, and by ourselves as the practitioners of this work.

Creativity

So, what is creativity? There have been many serious efforts, often wrought with tensions and difficulties, to define creativity. Creativity researchers have struggled, as creativity itself is not a concrete or immediately identifiable phenomenon (Mumford & Gustafson, 1988), and because creativity differs among peoples, societies, and cultures. The received definition states creativity is "the production of ideas which are both novel and useful" (Sternberg & Lubart, 1999, p. 3). However, Klausen (2010) argues against this definition and its rigidity, stating that it should be possible to engage in a creative process for the experience of the process itself, without the need for a tenable, novel, or useful result.

Winnicott (1971) was the first psychoanalyst to explicitly distinguish the role of creativity in the production of artwork from the artwork itself. Winnicott stipulates that the creative impulse is a thing in itself, involved in everyday creative living as much as in the production of artworks themselves (Glover, 2009). Therefore, there is no distinction in his mind between baking a cake, humming a tune, or composing a symphony. Neither, for that matter, is there any distinction between a work of art and an ordinary object. In this way, it is Winnicott who might be the most helpful to us when thinking about our own creativity in therapy, because he presents a level playing field in which "anything goes" and creative process is forefronted rather than product.

In 1953, Stein expressed that creativity must be defined and measured within its cultural context, yet it is only in more recent years that the cultural aspects of creativity have been studied. The majority of these studies have looked at the implicit and measurable aspects of creativity. In terms of the measurement of creativity, the main criticism appears to lie in the fact that Western tools, based on the concept of Western notions of creativity, are being used to assess creativity in other cultural settings. However, implicit theories—what people assume about creativity—are noted to be helpful in eliciting commonly held views on creativity, and in understanding what creativity means to people within a given community (Rudowicz, 2003).

Studies of culture specific conceptions of creativity indicate over-laps and differences in different cultural traditions, as well as differences in the value given to creative ventures and creativity. Of interest to family therapists is Csikszentmihalyi's (1988) adopting of a systems perspective on creativity, stating that to fully understand a person's behaviour, the person needed to be viewed as part of a system of mutual influence and information. Within this, it was acknowledged that the social, historical, and cultural context in which the individual functions affects the development and expression of creativity. As Csikszentmihalyi (1988, 1990) proposed, creativity is a process result-ing from three forces: culture, social system, and individual. It is culture which influences what is expressed, by whom, and how it is expressed. It also determines the function of the expression and the consequences to both individual and society (Ludwig, 1992). Therefore, when we consider working creatively with a family through any means, words, music, art, or drama, consideration of culture is important, with family therapists needing to embrace myriad cultural interfaces.

East and West concepts of creativity show a cross-cultural agree-ment that a creative product has to be useful, satisfactory, or deemed appropriate by a group. However, as Rudowicz (2003) observes, the concept of novelty and newness that fits with Western belief systems regarding individuality, democracy, and freedom contrasts to Eastern ideals of interdependence, collectivity, co-operation, and authoritari-anism. In Eastern cultures, an individual can come up with a new idea or product but must, at the same time, adhere to her social and cultural system and traditions. Therefore, creativity does not mean unconformity, but, rather, adaption and modification (Khleefa et al., 1996). This is similar to the concept of newness in African culture not holding special value: for example, a "new" ceremonial mask must contain certain "old" characteristics (Ludwig, 1992). This is in keeping with African innovations being concerned primarily with improvements—not inventions—aimed at developing existing tradition, as is also the concept of "renovation", perceived as a form of intellectual revision, which can pave the way for continuation of culture in a new, transformed form (Khleefa et al., 1996). The scope of modification and adaptation depends on the perceived threat of the creative endeavour to the religious, and political order and social norm. For example, within indigenous Afro–Arab culture, new ideas that conform to moral and religious values are more readily acceptable. In China, the concept of creativity is also bound with good morality and sociability (Liu et al., 1997), as can be seen in Chinese art education, which is as much about artistic expression as a means of moral education as it is about acquisition of skill (Gardner, 1989). Likewise, in Kenya, story-telling is left to the elders to ensure good ethical insight (Gacheru et al., 1999).

Generally, Western approaches to creativity are logical, look out towards progress through problem solving, and are happy to abandon information that does not "fit", due to an inherent demand that everything must fit together (Wonder & Blake, 1992). In comparison, Eastern approaches to creativity are "intuitive" and look inwards towards inner peace and what is already imbued in culture; within this, patterns of experience are rearranged, not abandoned. This concept is in keeping with early reflections in Chapter One, "A musical journey with Alice Brown", in which I argue the case for remaking experience rather than changing it in order not to abandon or ignore what might be fruitful from past experience.

In North America, research has found creativity to be related to concepts of humour and aesthetic appreciation. These implicit theories were non-existent in China, Hong Kong, and Taiwan, whose implicit theories of "inspires people", "makes a contribution to the progress of society", and "is appreciated by others" were, in turn, non-existent in their North American counterparts (Chan & Chan, 1999; Rudowicz & Yue, 2000). It is also important to note that, within an individual culture, gender differences towards notions of what creativity is are also evident. For example, female British teachers describe creativity as "self-expression" and "awareness of beauty", whereas male teachers describe creativity more objectively as "innovation" and "divergence"

(Fryer & Collins, 1991). It is, therefore, important when we approach a creative task in therapy to consider what we believe creativity is, how we think this might be organised by our gender and culture, and how this affects our approach.

The concept of creativity is influenced by its socio–historical context and the value given to the endeavour. It would appear that "people in every culture, even the progressive ones, are to some extent entrenched in a complicated set of human relationships and traditions, and creativity may pose a danger to these very relationships and practices" (Rudwicz, 2003, p. 280). Cultural contexts influence both the development of creativity in certain domains, and which domains are perceived as creative. This can be seen throughout each nation and within the micro workings of organisations with broad differences but also similarities. In this book, what permits and inhibits creativity within the family therapy space emerges as a central theme in the practitioners' experiences of using the music and art techniques.

Individuals such as Keeney (2009), a systemic psychotherapist and professor at the Department of Transformative Inquiry in San Francisco, make the case for inspiration and inventiveness, rather than theory, method, or technique being what awakens meaningful and transformative therapy. Keeney, who, in his classes, insists on discussing novels and fiction over professional texts, believes that an individual's "awakened heart" is necessary for therapy to be authentically transformative, and that relationship and mothering constitute the soul of therapy as opposed to "jousting interpretations" (p. xii). While I would agree that inspiration is joyous and transformative when we experience it within our practice, and I would agree that relationship is the core of what we do, I think that systemic psychotherapy has developed beyond projections of therapy as mothering towards more universally gender unspecific ideas concerning relationship. I also believe inspiration and inventiveness are only possible when we have embraced the richness inherent in theory and method. Once mastered, this theory creates the safe platform for development and creativity. Therefore, in terms of the techniques presented in this book, it is by following a few basic principles, initially, that your heart may become awakened to new possibilities.

Keeney believes that therapists are at their most creative when they draw upon their natural resources, gifts, and talents, and believes the life of being a creative therapist is inseparable from being a creative human being: "Awakening our clinical work requires revitalising our presence in everyday life" (p. 249). This book asks you to bring both your personal and professional self to the table, and invites you to tap into your own natural resources. Keeney could be viewed as adhering more closely to Eastern ideas that regard creativity as intuitive and looking inwards, in contrast to Western ideas of creativity that looks outward towards progress through problem solving, as could be said of the founders of family therapy. I believe we can hold a "both–and" position through allowing personal and professional aspects of ourselves to segue into practice more freely.

In this book, I am looking at the application of music and art in practice with the hope that this might reawaken family therapists' sense of family therapy as a context in which to be playful and creative. This book follows in the footsteps of others who have looked towards the creative arts for inspiration. For example, Wiener and Oxford (2003) have written on creative arts' improvisation in clinical practice, especially through drama and play, and Lowenstein (2010) has created a handbook of creative family therapy techniques using play, art, and expressive activities.

Keeney states that

> All therapists . . . live in a word mess, piles of theories strewn here and there, with a tractor in the front yard that hasn't tilled any soil for a long while. But somewhere inside you is a box of creative treasure just waiting to be opened and placed on your stage. (Keeney, 2009, p. 293)

I thought my treasure was music, but, while tilling the soil, I also came across art. I then realised that neither art nor music could be creative on their own; they are merely the tools to act as a conduit for my own creativity. Therefore, within the research that formed this book, it became important to instil awareness in family therapists of their own creativity while giving them some ideas and tools to help start this process.

CHAPTER THREE

Professional contexts: music and art therapy

T o use the non-verbal methods in family therapy that are presented in this book is to create a psychotherapy segue from family and systemic thinking to the music and art therapy professions. It is, therefore, important to understand the roots and development of work with families in these contexts, and to consider our "starting block" from a family therapy perspective in order to question where music and art have been used to date in family therapy, by whom, for what, and how?

Art and music therapy are divisions of psychotherapy where art or music is the primary communication method. These professions are born from a psychoanalytical tradition and do not offer a simple alternative to verbal interaction, but instead harness all the inherent healing properties of the arts (Linesch, 1999). Although there can be directive elements in music as well as art therapy, both professions work on the premise that the music or art is created from an act of communication or self-expression. While daunting for some, the physical blank canvas in art therapy can provide a sense of containment. Feelings can be held within the bounds of the canvas itself, which can act as an emotional container. In art therapy, it is the therapist's role to witness and be in conversation, as led by the client. In music therapy, clients are encouraged to musically improvise, and the therapist's role is to support, reflect, contain, and be in dialogue musically with what the client creates. There has always been debate within these professions over whether art is therapy itself, or art is something used in therapy for therapeutic means; whether music is therapy itself, or music is a means to an end and a way to reach a therapeutic objective. Many therapists hold dearly to one camp or the other, while others appreciate both positions. It is my belief that one is not possible without the other. Music, in its nature, can be therapeutic but can also meet clinical objectives. In writing this book, I was interested in specific techniques developed by the art and music therapy professions that can be adapted for use with families in the family therapy setting.

Music therapy and families

Integrating music into family therapy is not a new phenomenon. In 1991, Anthony Decuir, an American music therapist, attempted an overview of literature in his paper "Trends in music and family therapy". The result, although limited, is an important reference to the beginnings of thinking around the use of music with families. Feelings and affective material can be masked more easily with traditional verbal methods than through the arts, and, as a result, the need for comparative research of arts therapies *vs.* verbal therapies is highlighted.

The majority of writing up to 1991 concerning music therapy and families explored music therapy in the treatment of specific illness, and how family work became integrated into that arena. Areas cited are terminal illness, paediatric disorders, adult and adolescent psychiatry, autism, learning disability, and special needs. Most examples focus on hospitalised clients where music is used to help promote communication among family members. Early papers include McDonnell (1984), who describes using music therapy to help severely injured children and their families deal with events surrounding an accident and its aftermath, and Bailey (1984), who discusses the use of songs in music therapy with cancer patients and their families.

The most common use of music therapy with families is to facilitate communication among family members (Decuir, 1991; Hibben,

1992). As Hibben suggests, music can attract both children and adults, and instruments arouse curiosity as well as being removed from the negative connotations of toys. Specific attention is paid to music as "directed play" and the inclusion of improvisation techniques, as described by Bruscia (1987). Songs are considered an opportunity for intimate sharing between generations to communicate stories, illuminating positive and negative associations while strengthening alliances. These findings lead to a call for an investigation into the cross-cultural implications of using music therapy with families, as well as exploration into music therapy techniques that meet structural, strategic, and systemic methods of family therapy.

In response to Hibben, Miller (1994) set out to begin to build a foundation for integrating music therapy with primary, yet divergent, philosophical schools of family therapy. It is the first time that music therapy is considered from a family therapy perspective rather than a music therapy perspective. Specific music activities are proposed to allow a family to experience change within a session while addressing systemic, structural, and strategic family therapy objectives. The family is viewed as a system, with each family member playing a role in the functioning of the system and any change effecting the entire system. In this context, musical intervention is viewed as effective in encouraging self-expression, enhancing family communication skills and addressing structural imbalances of power within the family. The neutral nature of music is seen to potentially speed up the process of developing healthier communication patterns, without the distractions of content: for example, the resolution of arguments, as, although music is composed of the elements of speech, it does not carry the specific associations of words. This concept is explored further in Chapter Four.

From the 1990s through to the twenty-first century, a group of predominantly British female music therapists (Edwards, 2011; Oldfield, 1993, 1999, 2006; Oldfield & Bunce, 2001; Oldfield & Flower, 2008; Palmer, 1998, 2002; Warwick, 1995; Woodward, 2004) led the discourse around family work in music therapy in England, with a specific interest in mother and child work. The leaders in this thinking were Oldfield and Bunce (2001), who believe music therapy can be used as an effective intervention with parents who have difficult relationships with their children. Mother and baby interactions are described as being similar to child/client and therapist interaction, and music therapy is seen to allow older children to go back to a pre-verbal stage in order to re-create basic sound responses. Children are given the opportunity to re-experience, or experience for the first time, early mother–baby interactions as well as giving parents the opportunity to play and be playful. This correlates with my reflections on the case study in Chapter One of this book, "A musical journey with Alice Brown".

Further afield, Allgood (2005) researched family group music for children with autism, and McIntyre (2009) created the term "interactive family music therapy" to describe her work at Redbank House, a parent and child assessment centre in Australia. Parents and children attend the centre for an intensive one- or two-week stay. In this context, music therapy is used for assessment and treatment planning. Like Oldfield (2006), McIntyre is concerned with the interaction between family members, rather than between therapist and client. She describes the benefits of this approach as giving the family the opportunity to be part of intergenerational music making, where developmental age is respected and families are given the opportunity to engage in an activity together, maybe for the first time in a long while, which might be the catalyst for further conversations. The hope is for the family therapy space to be perceived as a fun and relaxing time where the family can play and speak more freely than in a verbal only session. In this way, a family can be part of an experience that could provide more immediate access to family processes than words. Australian policy and practice is used by Williams and colleagues (2014) as their starting point. They argue the case not only for music therapy, but employing the music therapist's skill set to help reach government policy objectives in the areas of hard to reach families, home visiting as assertive outreach, and integrated service delivery. In this way, systemic consideration is given to the wider context of practice as well as the practice itself.

In America, Nemesh (2017a) has expanded the use of "family-based music therapy" to offer music therapy to "non-clinical" families seeking therapy. Family-based music therapy adds a systems perspective to sessions. The work addresses family challenges while accessing the resources and strengths of the family, and focuses on interactions and communications between family members rather than on the individual. Music therapy research is expanded beyond parent–child dyads, family group interventions, and families of children with additional needs to "spotlight the family as an entity" (Nemesh, 2017a, p. 168). The work of Juliette Alvin, music therapy pioneer, is wedded to that of Virginia Satir, family therapy pioneer, to discuss how "the basic therapeutic attributes of musical improvisation such as attunement, mutuality and individuation are also core aspects of family functioning" (p. 168). It is an exciting development, but I would challenge Nemesh's statement that specialised training would be needed for family therapists to incorporate music into their practice. In this book, I propose that words are just as risky and potentially harmful as other forms of communication and that, at times, music can be a safer vehicle. Training in the use of music for family therapists would be rich and valuable, but it is not a prerequisite to exploring how music may enhance practice. Music cannot be owned by one profession; it is a universal gift for all to share. In a later paper, discussed below, Nemesh (2017b) does share this view and cites Ruud (2010), who calls for disciplines other than music therapy to embrace music as part of their toolkit.

The theoretical and practical use of systemic approaches in music therapy, and merging of systemic thinking and doing with music therapy practice, is also considered by Cobbett (2016). In Cobbett's approach, each discipline informs the other to create opportunities for increased understanding and positive change to be realised. Working with older children, in the less explored domain of social, emotional, and behavioural difficulties, he sees music making as highlighting relational difficulties in the family, creating a healthy social activity to nurture positive interactions, and as a conduit for celebrating the family's culture. Although cross-cultural implications for music therapy have been discussed in the music therapy field (Bruscia, 1998; Forrest, 2014; Pavlicevic, 1997; Stige, 2002), specific examples of using music therapy with a family in a clinical setting all originate in the Western literature reviewed above. "Music therapy" is a Western construct: in Africa, for example, music therapy could be described as a phenomenon that envelops all areas of culture and day-to-day life. Here, in society, there is no distinction between performers and audience, and therapy is administered in non-clinical settings by herbalists, witch-doctors, and faith healers. Family and community are also interlinked by strong connections and meanings absent from Western society. They have no need for a separate clinical setting to see if music can help families in crisis, because music is already integral to their existence and already playing its part in birth, strife, healing, and death (Aluede, 2006).

Music therapy, like all therapy, has a responsibility to embrace cultural difference and Forrest (2014), in a beautiful article outlining the cultural intricacies of her work, calls for culturally responsive practice in which music therapists must consider "the cultural *song* of the family; their own cultural *song*; and how, through both their similarities and differences, they can come together to create a *new song*" (p. 27). This resonates with how I wish you to approach the techniques described later in this book.

In 2012, Oldfield and colleagues reflected on short-term music therapy in child psychiatry and describe family work as still relatively unusual. However, four years later, in discussing the development of music therapy services in the NHS, Wood and colleagues (2016) speak of it being standard practice in their NHS Trust to include parents in the music therapy room, with children being seen alone as a much more unusual occurrence. Albeit the focus appears often to be with younger children, what is clear is that there is a changing climate in music therapy to include family as standard practice in sessions, or, at least, consider the inclusion of parents. With these changes, I believe the professions of music therapy and family therapy are being brought closer together, and hope for sharing, learning, and growth to be developed consequently.

Family therapy and music

Although live music making in the family therapy space appears rare, musical ideas have been discussed through metaphor, as can be seen in Hills' (2006) use of musical language to describe Minuchin's work, calling family therapists not to be prejudiced by a first reaction but to "listen to the music underneath", as Minuchin is "intuitive, playful, humorous and able to use language with nuance and subtlety in seeking strengths and resources" (p. 228). The use of Louis Armstrong's music in a session with family therapy trainees is described, as an example of how jazz music broke the mould and contributed to the liberation of an oppressed and discriminated sector of the population. The music speaks and tells a story.

Helping trainees tell a story through creative descriptions was also invited by McLean and colleagues (1999), who illustrate how one student called Martha brought in three musicians to her family therapy examination who performed a "jam" session with her to describe her experience of family therapy. Pre-recorded music has also found a place in family therapy as an agent for promoting discussion around personal and interpersonal conflicts (Hendricks & Bradley, 2005; Man Keung Ho & Settles, 1984), alongside a belief that a family's perception of the real world might be reflected in their choice of music and is a part of cultural and ethnic identity (Mickel & Mickel, 2002). Music is seen as one of the essential communicative components of most environments, and family therapists are encouraged to work "within the real world" with attention being brought to the importance of lyrics through the example of rap music.

In thinking about couple work, Fraenkel (2011), couple and family therapist and professional jazz drummer, uses the concept of musical rhythm as a metaphor to describe couple arrhythmia, stating that partners frequently complain of feeling "out of sync" with each other. The aim is to help couples to assess and change the specific ways that time differences between each other contribute to relational distress.

More recently, specific exercises for family therapists to use in sessions have been available: for example, Lowenstein (2010) includes exercises such as the "family orchestra" and "rappin' family puppet interview" in her book, *Creative Family Therapy Techniques: Play, Art and Expressive Activities to Engage Children in Family Sessions*. In "family orchestra", body sounds such as foot stomping and hand clapping are used to make short pieces of music that follow the beat of a drum. The person with the drum is the leader and various games are created around the activity. In "rappin' family puppet interview", Sori (2008) musically and culturally adapts "the family puppet interview" (Gil, 1994; Irwin & Malloy, 1974) inviting families to write their story as a rap.

This book is based on research (Palmer, 2014) that includes reflections on family therapists' perceptions of using music and art in their practice. Subsequently, Nemesh (2017b), a dual-trained music therapist and family therapist, has also conducted research to elucidate family therapists' perspectives on using musical interventions in family therapy. From a sample of thirty-five family therapists working in Israel, her results illustrate that family therapists feel less knowledgeable and skilled in music than other expressive arts and most family therapists never use music. She discovered that visual arts are used almost twice as often as other expressive arts, due to their familiarity, accessibility, and more ready use in education. Visual arts were also seen as less revealing and less chaotic, with negative cultural attitudes towards noise and the practical implications of cost and storage of instruments being reasons therapists would choose not to use music. Nemesh's results corroborate the responses I received from initial interviews I conducted in my research, before I had taught family therapists music and art techniques. Nemesh found that 71% of her participants approached the idea of using music in their work positively and talked of being curious and excited at the experimental qualities of music to bridge communication. A further 23% had a mixed response and harboured self-doubt, fearing their lack of skill, the unfamiliarity of music, and the possibility of interrupting the family therapy process, and only 2% felt using music in family therapy was nonsense and not applicable to practice. In my research, as you will read in Chapters Five and Nine, I had no participants who expressed this view, and although similar feelings of self-doubt and fears of appearing ridiculous were expressed, this was to change following the participants' own experience of using music in a workshop setting. What both Nemesh's and my research point to is an exciting changing climate within family therapy towards exploring creative difference.

Art therapy and families

The beginnings of art family therapy started with the work of Kwiatkowska (1978), who worked at the National Institute for Mental Health in Maryland. Kwiatkowska was a close colleague of Wynne, who developed the family art evaluation approach (FAE), an adaptation of an earlier diagnostic assessment for individuals (Ulman, 1975). The FAE concentrates on four concepts congruent with family therapy: life cycle, communication/behaviour, structure, and unconscious family life. As the family moves through a series of tasks in the FAE, a multi-dimensional "portrait" emerges that elucidates the family's unique relational experience (Sobol & Williams, 2001).

Family art therapy, as an approach, has developed along a similar path to family systems theory (Bowen, 1978) with both Bowen and

Kwiatkowska's work emanating from their observations of the families of their schizophrenic clients. Kwiatkowska believed the family is less guarded in art therapy than in verbal situations. Anger and hostility can be expressed without such intense feelings of guilt, and family members are often able to accept their real perception of themselves and others through art more readily than through words. Following Kwiatkowska, other art assessments were also developed for couples (Wadison, 1973), families with young children (Rubin & Magnussen, 1974) and whole families (Landgarten, 1987). Sobol and Schneider (1996) point to a wealth of art therapy techniques that have been devised for use with families which range from family murals (Rubin, 1978) to magazine collages (Landgarten, 1987; Linesch, 1999), construction projects (Riley & Malchiodi, 1994; Sobol & Schneider, 1996) to work in clay (Keyes, 1984; Kwiatkowska, 1978).

In contrast to the music therapy profession, the art therapy profession has made explicit attempts to keep up with ongoing trends in family therapy. Whereas the music therapy profession generally stops at modern ideas and comparisons in terms of their family therapy thinking, the art therapy world continues the journey into postmodern ideas. Carlson (1997) believes narrative therapy (White & Epston, 1990) and art therapy share certain theoretical beliefs in recapturing hidden aspects of lived experience, adhering to the principal of co-construction in understanding the therapeutic relationship, and the overall belief in the creative abilities of people.

Integrating art therapy techniques into a narrative approach was developed by Carlson (1997), who specifically looked at four major concepts: discovering dominant stories, externalisation, unique outcomes, and performing before an audience. In thinking about bringing forth dominant stories, Carlson has discovered self-portraits (Wadison, 1973) are an effective tool to help clients tell their stories. In terms of externalisation, Carlson believes that for a client to draw their problem is a very dramatic way to separate the problem from his life, and describes it as externalisation in the most literal sense. For unique outcomes, Carlson believes that art can serve the same purpose as letter writing in narrative therapy to amplify alternative stories. Last, in thinking about the need for an audience to tell the story to, art provides the opportunity to rehearse the story and new relationship to the problem, with the outcome being that the client is able to both tell a story and present a new picture of themselves to the audience.

Offering opportunities to do art in family therapy is offering a task to be done in the here and now, which might be a concept absent in the work of many family therapists who concentrate on the spoken word and what is inherent in conversation. To counter this, Riley (2000) offers a useful and user-friendly presentation of art family therapy. Riley believes if there is chaos in the system, the family should be offered the opportunity to organise themselves around a task. She finds it useful, in the first session, to ask a family to represent the issue that they personally see as the family's problem. This allows all members to have a voice and not need to struggle with words. In the activity itself, a mini enactment of the family's way of relating is displayed. This helps to avoid or reduce parental blaming of the adolescent and an onslaught of problem-saturated dialogue.

From the start of therapy, assigning the family tasks sends a message that working together is a goal. A family mural, in which each member of the family draws with a separate colour so each individual's journey within the family exercise can be traced, is suggested by Riley. It is a powerful tool that can immediately present a graphic depiction of family dynamics. The therapist's role is as observer and witness and allows the therapist the opportunity to observe the family's structure, assigned roles, behavioural patterns, communication systems, and styles. This is also described as "the family drawing" (Linesch, 1999) which comes from an extensive tradition of family art therapy (Kwiatkowska, 1978; Landgarten, 1981; Riley & Malchiodi, 1994). The therapist's taking of a "not knowing" approach is helpful in a collaborative puzzling out of meanings and understanding. It is believed that this allows for concealed issues to more readily surface than through verbal methods (Riley, 2000).

It has been argued that children have, to a large extent, been excluded from full participation in family therapy sessions (Lund et al., 2002) and, in an effort to address this, Shafer (2008) has created arts-based family therapy resources which are structured and directive in format. In thinking about families with young children, Kozlowska and Hanney (1999) devised a family assessment and intervention exercise from a synthesis of clinical tools used by attachment theorists and family art therapists, in the knowledge that when non-verbal communication is used, young children's participation in sessions is four times greater than when only verbal communication is used (Cederborg, 1997). The exercise involves three steps: first, the family are asked to draw a picture of themselves, and then the self-portraits are cut out and put on a sheet of paper to form a family picture, second, the family are given a lump of clay and asked to create a castle, magic cave, or forest, and last, they are asked to create a collage together depicting a family day out. From these activities, information is gathered on roles, boundaries, alliances, development, interactions, and perceptions.

Art interventions have the potential to parallel many of the theoretical paradigms of family therapy (Kerr & Hoshino, 2008). In their book, *Family Art Therapy*, Kerr and Hoshino set out to create a family art therapy text that brings together classic and postmodern family therapy theories and techniques with art therapy approaches. For example, enactment through structural family art therapy takes place through the process of collaborative art creation. However, the therapist concentrates on the process over the content of the family painting, and looks for ways to realign and strengthen boundaries through observations and practical interventions, such as changing family positions around the table.

In researching how family therapists might begin to incorporate art and music into a systemic approach, the arts therapy professions are an invaluable resource in providing practical techniques which have been tried and tested. This is especially true of the art therapy profession where family art therapy has an established position within art therapy practice and will be called on in the presentation of techniques in Chapter Eight.

Family therapy and art

To incorporate art into practice is to accept that there are diverse ways of seeing. When Woodcock (2003) discusses Berger's (1972) *Ways of Seeing*, he invites our imagination to enter a world where images, not language, provide our primary sense of being in the world. Embracing this way of seeing might shine a light on how family therapists respond to using art in sessions, not to interpret and explain, but to observe and notice, remaining attentive, attuned, and offering containment and connectedness. This process is described as an emerging of less conscious aspects of experience finding expression: "through art, sensation, and eventually language" (Woodcock, 2003, p. 235).

As family therapy models began to stress process over content, the active techniques that arts therapists (drama, dance, art) used, became popular (Landgarten, 1991): for example, rehearsals of interactions, drawings as representational of feelings, and expressive activity presenting a family's basic communication patterns. Art and family therapy approaches were combined by Manicom and Boronska (2003), who conclude that art provides channels of communication that might not otherwise be accessed, allowing children to play an active role using a media that they believe is more accessible and safer than words.

It has been argued by Carlson (1997) that there is a rationale for the integration of art therapy and narrative therapy ideas in order to aid the deconstructive process of narrative therapy. In thinking about narrative therapy (White & Epston, 1990), Carlson argues that the principles of art therapy and narrative therapy fit together theoretically, and can be used to help families bring forth dominant stories, externalise their difficulties, create unique outcomes, and perform before an audience. The importance of the family having a picture has been emphasised by Epston and colleagues (1992) as "one must have a convincing picture to show others" (p. 111). This picture to show others is viewed as a powerful tool for change (Zimmerman & Sheppard, 1993). Cartoons have also been used, as described by Ball and colleagues (1993). They believe that cartoons can add to the externalisation process, linking with the culture of childhood, and demonstrate that it does not matter how the picture is executed and what form it takes, but how that process is supported and what is communicated to the audience of self, family, and therapist. This joins with the idea that "it is not enough to just tell a new story to ourselves, there must be a performance to a relevant audience" (Epston et al., 1992, p. 98).

In terms of dialogical thinking, Rober (2009) has devised a protocol for using relational drawings as a dialogical tool for use in couple therapy: "it offers the couple a mirror that is not blaming, but rather invites them to try and listen generously to each other" (p. 132). In Rober's work, it is the dialogical exchange around the drawings that is central, rather than the content, and drawing is given as a homework task, not a task conducted within a family therapy session.

Multi-family group work, developed since the 1960s (Laquer et al., 1964; Strelinck, 1977) is now readily used as a therapeutic intervention to provide families with the opportunity to convene together in a structured programme, to gain multi-perspectives on their situation, find support, and gain resources for recovery or managing symptoms and their consequences (Asen, 2002). Multi-family group work first concentrated on schizophrenic patients and their families but is now used in many other presentations and conditions, for example, eating disorders (Dare & Eisler, 2000; Scholtz & Asen, 2001; Slagerman & Yager, 1989), drug and alcohol abuse (Kaufman & Kaufmann, 1981) and chronic medical illness (Steinglass, 1998). A three-day multi-family group programme for eating disordered patients is described by Colahan & Robinson (2002) that combines creative or experiential sessions with verbal sessions. Included in the creative sessions is an art therapy workshop. In the workshop, families are requested to illustrate together a family event on a large piece of paper and the example is shared of four families involved in the programme, all drawing a representation of a family meal when asked to do this exercise. Three families drew a bright, colourful picture and one family drew a stark black and white picture evoking the harsh realities of anorexia. The families who had drawn the three idealised colourful pictures were shaken by the black and white image and their denial of the brutality of anorexia. These families had been impervious to the therapist's attempts to help them be realistic about their situation; it was only the image created and shared by the fourth family that was able to act as a powerful catalyst to free the group to think more creatively and realistically.

There is a rich and abundant collection of creative ideas and techniques in Lowenstein's book, *Creative Family Therapy Techniques* (2010), for use in family therapy. The techniques use play, games, drama, and art to aid the inclusion of children in family therapy sessions and offer alternate ways to communicate and interact. Lowenstein's activities of "messages in art" devised by Lori Gill, and "walk a mile in my shoes", contributed by Alison Smith, strike a chord with this book. In "messages in art" each person in the family is asked to choose a person they would like to send a message to. Family members are then asked to visualise the feelings behind the message before creating their message through the art materials. The individual is then asked to explain their message to the recipient. This links with a general theme that runs throughout the art techniques presented in Chapter Eight of this book, about colours, feelings, and different perceptions and understanding being gained through a shared art activity. "Walk a mile in my shoes" is also like the "footprints" exercise included in Chapter Eight. In "Walk a mile" Smith asks family members to swap shoes and then go on a walk around the room or up the hall. When in the shoes, family members are asked to "be" the person whose shoes they are in and then report back on the experience.

Summary

As the music and art therapy professions have embraced work with families and family therapy thinking, so, too, has the family therapy profession been considering how the use of non-verbal media can enhance creativity in practice. What we see is a grappling within the family therapy profession to find a theoretical fit to justify the use of something other than words. What I would argue is that using music and art is about offering an alternative way of communicating and seeing the world; the emphasis should be on process and experience, and not too closely wedded to finding a fit with existing theory.

CHAPTER FOUR

A shared humanity: music, words, and the mind

I am curious to understand more fully whether and how the use of music and art in family therapy not only changes the families' perceptions of each other, but might also change therapists' ways of thinking around the difficulties and dilemmas they face in their practice. I am interested in how right brain experiences can be developed in the therapy environment, both for the families and for the therapists working with the families, in order for therapy to be experienced as a *Gestalt*, a whole entity. It is my belief that, as therapists with words as our main tool, we understandably can become left brain dominant, logical, and analytical, when, in fact, it is positive and flexible right brain emotions we are trying to elicit, such as hope and forgiveness.

If music is a vital way of binding society in a shared humanity which actively draws people together (McGilchrist, 2009), I am left questioning what our societal and cultural context is when convening families in crisis and offering opportunities to play music or interact using art. Can it appeal to a lost sense of communion with each other and the wider world, a shared humanity? If so, how might this change the relationship between therapist and family? And what is it in the music itself, as well as the process of playing, or in the co-creation of a piece of art, that can activate new ways of thinking?

Music, art, and the brain

The concept that both hemispheres of the brain are involved in every-day activity but each hemisphere has its own specialisation, and processes information in its own way, was developed by Sperry and colleagues (1969). The left brain, with its externally focused, linear, verbal, and analytical processes, is thought to be the largely dominant hemisphere, due to its language component, and also has its own role in the creative process (Zdenek, 1988). However, in order to internally focus, the right brain induces the ability to be sensitive to intonations of voice and body, to comprehend symbols and metaphors, and to think visually, holistically, and imaginatively. The work of Sperry and colleagues (1969) was to inspire the artist and teacher Betty Edwards (1979) to investigate why it was that some of her pupils could draw and others struggled. Edwards realised that a shift from verbal analyt-ical processing, which she referred to as "left mode", to spatial global processing "right mode" aided the drawing process. As a result, she designed a series of drawing exercises to tap into the special functions of the right hemisphere, which she states, "have empirically been proven to be successful with students at all levels and therefore hold up irrespective of how strictly lateralized the brain mechanisms might be" (p. vii).

In terms of the origins of music, there is a tentative link to music being originally created in response to the sounds of nature (Storr, 1992), but there are stronger links to the idea that music was created in response to the verbal/sound exchanges that go on between a mother and child in the first year of life, as these exchanges are about emotional content, reflection, and validation, rather than conveying factual information (Dissanayake, 1990). If so, the human brain is first organised to respond to emotional aspects of the human voice and, in this way, all non-sung music could perhaps be considered as songs without words. As Storr (1992) recognises, music can often be so dis-sociated from verbal meaning and, therefore, everything that comes with verbal reasoning that it can be experienced by some as the essence of life, and an experience that makes sense of life itself.

Since the 1980s, there has been a call not to differentiate too defin-itively between left and right brain function, as evidence shows they do work together (Loye, 1983). However, there has also been growing evidence (Horton, 1988) that the right brain is the locus of subjectively experienced positive feeling evoking states of joy, love, gratitude, pleasure, bliss, and happiness. These, in turn, may refer to behaviour as well as subjective experience such as surprise, altruism, interest, praise, hope, reassurance, forgiveness, and generosity. As McGilchrist (2009) emphasises, what we once thought went on in one hemisphere or the other alone is now known to go on in both; however, it would appear that the left hemisphere tends to deal more with pieces of information in isolation, whereas the right hemisphere deals with the whole. In terms of right and left hemisphere roles, there is evidence of left hemisphere dominance in local, narrowly focused attention and right hemisphere dominance for broad, global, and flexible attention. This difference can be summarised as: "two fundamentally different 'versions' delivered to us by the two hemispheres, both of which can have a ring of authenticity about them, and both of which are hugely valuable" (McGilchrist, 2009, p. 5). Information is constantly transferred between the two hemispheres of the brain, but each hemisphere has its own "take" on events, experiences, and understanding of the world. It is also the case that one hemisphere will certainly override the other hemisphere concerning certain activities, which can be seen in the right brain's stimulation from music and art.

Although music is not an exclusively right brain phenomenon, music's emotional content, including intonations of voice, mean that it is of special concern to the right hemisphere. Music is not an entity in isolation, but is about the relation between things; it is the relationship between the notes that creates the music, the notes mean nothing in themselves, and between the notes is silence without which the notes would not have meaning. The notes and the silence together create a whole (McGilchrist, 2009). Everything about music makes it the natural language of the right hemisphere, from its emotive communication to its embodied nature. As Miller (1994) describes, music is more stimulating than verbal dialogue because it stimulates a combination of visual, auditory, and kinaesthetic associations.

Music not only has the power to recall emotional states, but also to allow the performer or listener to experience emotional states they have not experienced before (Langer, 1942). Interestingly, although speech is primarily dominated in the left hemisphere, song is associated with the activation of the right hemisphere. Following a left hemisphere stroke, a patient could be left unable to speak, but able to sing the words of a song without difficulty. If language began in song rather than spoken words, it began in an empathic form, not a competitive one, promoting togetherness or "betweeness" (McGilchrist, 2009). In this way, human singing is unique, no other creature sings in the same way. Birdsong, by contrast, is individualistic and competitive. This theory connects to earlier thoughts in this book about Western and Eastern concepts of creativity and the role of culture. When I convened the family therapy participants for my research, they were all keen as long as no singing was required. Singing has become so detached from its empathic beginnings, and yet it is the most basic, but perhaps the most revealing, of human communication.

If music is linked to the initial sounds between mother and child, when we ask a parent and child to be in dialogue with each other through music in family therapy, we are, therefore, tapping into a primitive source of communication, removed from the complexities of language, to return to a basic way of interacting and being together. If we are to believe that music's emotional content, including intonations of voice, make it of special concern to the right hemisphere of the brain (McGilchrist, 2009), and that within the right hemisphere there is dominance for broad, global, and flexible attention, then the argument for utilising music in family therapy is supported, in order to stimulate interest and attentiveness on different levels, through stimulating brain activity. In contrast, language and the spoken word are located in the left hemisphere, which has dominance in local, narrowly focused attention.

In thinking about the brain and the musical activities presented in this book, it is important to note that tone, timbre, harmony, and pitch are almost always mediated via the right hemisphere and rhythm is more widely based. Metrical simple rhythms are especially left dominated, whereas more complex rhythms and syncopations are treated preferentially by the right hemisphere. This is pertinent to the "Beginnings" activities in Chapter Six that rely on shared rhythmic activities between therapist and family before considering pitch or harmony. However, the activities do invite more complex interweaving of rhythmic ideas early on in the development of the activity, which should, in turn, stimulate right brain activity. I am curious, if a family or therapist becomes stuck with this initial activity, whether it could be indicative of a left brain dominant relationship with the world. If so, it might be possible to initially use rhythm in its simplest metrical presentation as a bridge between left and right brain activity. These differentiations of hemispheric purpose apply to the amateur musician; the professional musician appears to use the left hemisphere to a much greater extent in the understanding of music (McGilchrist, 2009). This makes sense if considering the mathematical and academic processes involved in producing and analysing music. Therefore, if the therapist is faced with a family who are highly musically trained, I would suggest art as a starting point, rather than musical intervention, which could lead to more narrowly focused attention and competition, rather than a broader and more flexible way of experiencing interaction.

When I first began my research, a thought struck me as I was driving my car, so I stopped and wrote this on the back of an envelope: "The unbearable lightness of being. Can art and music allow a family to 'be'? To be in the present? To experience a 'now-ness' without recrimination? The art of doing nothing. Art and music are 'doing' things but the process allows for a sense of the here and now, a sense of being in the moment. Family therapy is often so busy. Does our talk distract away from the essence of what is happening? Is it too painful just to be? The therapist's own need to be doing. Can the therapist allow for just being?"

In my musings, what I was touching on was the idea of mindfulness. Mindfulness is the ability to intentionally bring awareness to the present moment without judgement (Kabat Zin, 1990) and is attributed to ancient Buddhist tradition, but can be seen in most faith traditions (Shapiro & Carlson, 2009). In healthcare, the teaching of mindfulness to clients dates from 1979, but thoughts on the importance of therapist *attention* date back to Freud, who stipulated the therapist needed to remain open to the present moment (Mace, 2007). In psychotherapy, mindfulness focuses on three areas: mindful based therapeutic interventions, mindfulness as a factor within the therapeutic alliance, and the influence of mindfulness in informing psychotherapy (Abbey, 2012). Mindful-based cognitive therapy and mindful-based stress reduction are common mindfulness-based therapies. Mindfulness is also a core concept in dialetical behaviour training and acceptance and commitment therapy (Shapiro & Carlson, 2009).

In Rappaport's (2014) book, *Mindfulness and the Arts Therapies*, specific attention is paid to the expansion of mindful practices within the psychotherapy field and how this intersects with developments in mindfulness within the arts therapies. As Kass and Trantham (2014) state, individuals who have lost touch with the visceral sensations and internal messages of their bodies, who have not gained accurate verbal access to their emotions, and who lack the reflexive capacity of an observing self, require experiential sensor-motor "bottom up" psychotherapy rather than predominantly verbal "top down" psychotherapy forms. (p. 305)

Such treatment provides: "pre-verbal somatic experiences of safety" and "increased sensorimotor awareness and somatic emotion-regulation skills that build tolerance" as well as "internal experience of a calm core; gradual movement to verbal capacities for self-disclosure and social engagement" (p. 305). However, this considers primarily the individual; how does it correlate to working with the whole family system?

Mindful-based family therapy has its roots in the early experiential work of Carl Whitaker and Virginia Satir, but draws mostly on contemporary mindful-based therapy, especially the Hakomi method and somatic experiencing (Lavie, 2011). The Hakomi method (Kurtz, 1990) uses mindful-based techniques to uncover and reshape core belief systems. Somatic experiencing (Levine, 2010) helps clients to manage internal experiences through tracking levels of arousal. Mindful based family therapy is about helping families to become aware of underlying experiences such as feelings, impulses, beliefs and bodily experiences in a way that "allows us to drop into the unknown, to bring the witnessing brain to experiences that have been invisible and automatic" (Lavie, 2011, p. 2). This allows us to get beneath the stories that family members tell themselves. In this way, we are activating the limbic brain, the part of the brain that is responsible for relationships and our emotional world.

I believe if we provide verbal and non-verbal opportunities in family therapy, there is the potential to create a safer, more tolerant, socially engaging forum to help unravel stuck family stories. I did not set out to create mindful art and music techniques in this book; however, the literature would suggest that the very use of art and music can create a more mindful state. The description "calm core" is associated with individuals. In my experience, the use of music and art helps establish and tap into the "calm core" of a family, allowing for alternative perspectives to be explored and realised.

Words, words, words

In *The Will to Power*, Nietzsche (1968) writes, "compared with music, communication by words is shameless; words dilute and brutalize; words depersonalize; words make the uncommon common" (pp. 427–428). When discussing "not saying what can't be said", Frosh (2007) describes the experience of many that language does not fully encompass or reflect reality and that, although we are positioned by the language we use, we often are left feeling we missed the point. When Hamlet responds to Polonious's question about what he is reading with the famous line "words, words, words", it could be argued that Hamlet, overwhelmed with angst and in existential crisis, has no words to describe his suffering.

Although the fact that we keep trying is a testament to the importance of language (indeed, Hamlet's other soliloquies are testament to that effort), Frosh believes the reason things cannot be said is that language leaves us with gaps and difference. This can be explained through the notion that there are too many ways of saying things, and to do justice to what we wish to express would be to use all these different ways at once. Also, language is continually transforming in relation to the other and "the speaking of the thing acts as a wager, a point at which something is risked into existence". Therefore, as we "pronounce upon experience so the experience must change" (Frosh, 2007, p. 641).

It could be argued that as language "constructs" our experience, music and art do the same, with the variations in the cultural use of art and music, as discussed in Chapter Two, shining a light on how cultural constructions are expressed through different artistic media. However, in thinking about Frosh's idea that as we "pronounce upon experience so the experience must change" (Frosh, 2007, p. 641), I am interested in the idea of risking something into existence and the incapacity of words to sometimes do that fully or correctly. I believe that is where non-verbal communication can "speak" in the place of words. I also believe that words can form a barrier between unconscious and conscious processes, as noted earlier when citing Bateson as saying, "too much consciousness may make impossible some desired sequence of events" (Hoffman, 1995, p. 44). In this way, words can get in the way of insight, intuition, and imagination finding expression. It is a fundamental belief of music and art therapy that the non-verbal processes employed bring together the domains of conscious and unconscious experience. Perhaps this is the biggest challenge, and the biggest opportunity, for the family therapist.

CHAPTER FIVE

Trying something new: thoughts from the starting line

I want to share some conversations with you that I had with therapists about music, art, and creativity before teaching them the techniques presented in this book. I hope that this will validate some of the feelings that you, as therapists, might experience on your own journey using music and art in your work, highlighting any pitfalls, and helping you with ideas to bolster and sustain your practice.

With a little help from Ella . . .

So, where does Ella Fitzgerald fit into the picture? Ella was a shy and retiring child, who grew up in poverty and suffered great loss at a young age. However, Ella could "sing how [she] feels" (Ella Fitzgerald). I have used music and art in my practice to help when young people struggle to find the words, or there are no words, to offer an alternative way of communicating thoughts and feelings. Therefore, it feels fitting to use Ella Fitzgerald song titles as subheadings to introduce each section.

Curiosity, excitement, and a desire to be creative

"Embraceable you"

All family therapists shared a desire to embrace the opportunity to learn some creative techniques and develop new ways of thinking about therapy.

> *Kay*: I thought it might reawaken my dulled creativity [laughter] ... so that's my hope really, to wake me up.

> *Esme*: I was thinking about the families that we see who aren't so verbal and maybe, you know, we can get stuck with developing ideas because they are restricted in how much they can articulate, so for me using different kinds of creative ways of exploring ideas is something interesting.

> *Leo*: For me it's also about having a toolbox of things that I can use, to use when I feel like it or when the moment is right, because the type of families we work with often have multiple problems, so that for a lot of the sessions it is very hard to plan.

Uncertainty, anxiety, and self-consciousness

"That certain feeling"

With many therapists, there was an element of vulnerability and anxiety about trying something new, including some strong feelings of constraint about opening into new areas of creative working.

> *Vanessa*: I feel constrained in myself, and I don't know where to take the conversation ... I struggle to incorporate it into what we are doing ... it's how you use what you are trying to create, to move things forward.

> *Linda*: I feel quite comfortable with arty things but the music thing, I'm sort of thinking, do you have to get out and start and play an instrument yourself or something? [Laughter.]

However, for others, who had music within their everyday cultural context, using music in the work setting was more of an enigma.

> *Harriet*: ... and I thought music we can't do, why don't we do it? You know, how could we do it? ... I was kind of interested in music being fun and, um, that was my initial thought, but then I thought music is so

moving you can use it in so many different ways and why don't we, why don't I?

Marcus: I think music feels quite exposing, which on the flip side might be a positive thing because you can actually bring yourself in more directly.

Marcus viewed opportunities to feel awkward and de-skilled as a potential isomorphic process that might help the family who feel equally anxious and de-skilled, in a similar way to one of the therapists in Chapter One, "A musical journey with Alice Brown". Marcus's idea questions our position as therapist with families; what we can risk and how introducing something new might need negotiating within the therapeutic relationship. For other therapists, introducing something different and feeling de-skilled was more threatening, as can be seen below.

A need to be taken seriously

"They all laughed"

Louise: There is something about families coming thinking that they are coming for talking and then you are introducing something else, and instruments, as you say, feels very different, too different [laughter].

Harriet: Is it too childish, you know? The parents might say why are we doing this? Is this real therapy? That might be what's holding me back.

Linda: It might be a really good medium for engaging with someone who finds talking quite difficult, but the sort of thought about how you might bring the music into a session without feeling ridiculous.

Therapists discussed what being "systemic" means and what it means to be working systemically. They concluded that, for family therapists, words are the safe base from which professional identity, therapeutic alliance, and efficacy are all strongly associated. Music and art, on the other hand, initially signified not only the unknown, but something potentially dangerous, that could see therapists exposed and at risk of compromising professional integrity. The conversation also constructed art and music as something strongly linked to a childhood or leisure activity that could disturb the peace with noise and mess, and, therefore, might not be conducive to the serious nature of therapy.

The confidence to be different

"Something's gotta give"

> Shulah: Well, I was quite anxious and would be the first to think "Oh God", but I do want to do it because I can see how valuable it is, you know, especially with adolescents I think, the expressing themselves through music and art, which I have never been able to do because I am not, I'm rubbish at art, so I was quite anxious thinking that, I'm very excited to learn.

It became evident that the concept of being creative might be a potential barrier to embracing the techniques. I came to understand that it is not only what you bring professionally, but what you bring personally that equally influences the ability to embed something different within professional practice. Professional practice, and, therefore, professional identity, was constructed as closely linked to knowledge and use of words in helping to create change. Therefore, the addition of something new that is not word based challenged that identity.

The concept of creativity

"Just one of those things"

> Elsbeth: Over the years I have done a lot of thinking and dipping a toe in the water of using more creative activities, and because I'm not confident in them in relation to myself, um, I lose confidence in trying to apply that with families. It does feel easier if you are just with children on your own, I guess, but it's also about my own confidence.

Therapists held two discrepant beliefs. The first belief was that art is accessible to all when thinking about the young people we work with; this is due to an assumption that all children can do art. The second belief was that due to individual differences in the "talents" or "creativity" of the therapist, access to art is restricted. Therefore, the belief in value and accessibility is overshadowed by individual and personal beliefs created in the historical and social contexts of most therapists, especially concerning the school experience.

> *Nadine*: The teacher went around and decided that there was someone singing off key, "There is definitely somebody singing off key" [laughter] and then came up to me and said, "It's you!" and "Don't sing any more."

Work pressures and organisational change

"Miss Otis regrets"

The therapists spoke about current struggles and pressures in working within the National Health Service.

> *Nadine*: I think when you are pressured you stick to your comfort zone; if art and music is less comfortable for us, it is not something we are going to rush to do and there is so much change going on, you just want to stay in your contained little world . . .

Therapists' experience of work pressures resulted in limited time for thinking and organising alternative activities. In this context, therapists return to what feels safe and what they know. Described by therapists as the 'comfort position', this defaulting process can be both a natural response to work pressures and risk, as well as key to understanding the process of change.

In this book, the idea of challenging organisational culture is posed. The challenge is about doing something differently, not necessarily talking about the "doing", with the hope of igniting people's curiosity around difference.

> *Harriet*: I was thinking about the constraints of the building, which we talked about here . . . I was just thinking [laughter], in our CAMHS team I think it would arouse a lot of curiosity, people will want to know what's going on.

The importance of team support

"Day in day out"

The influence of team culture was identified, with therapists needing their teams to work with them if they were to embrace something new.

Therapists found it helpful to latch on to the creativity of others and stressed the importance of new ideas being accepted and supported by the team if they were to survive:

> *Sharon*: It's not something you can suddenly do in the middle of a session, let's turn it into a music or an art session, you've got to get it planned ahead I think, it does help to have a team where you are all working together on it.

Music and art were seen as being used in quite a formal, planned way in multi-family therapy and the planning was seen as making it possible for it to work. However, multi-family work is very different from working with individual families. The techniques in this book are flexible and adaptable tools. It might be that you feel the need to plan initially, but try not to be too wedded to any plan, just as we would not approach a family with a list of questions.

The nature of childhood

"Reaching for the moon"

It was believed that children give us permission to be curious and, as children are not necessarily aware of rules and restrictions, this can be freeing. While children have permission to be free, curious, and creative, adults were seen as being constrained by rules. Children respond naturally and it was experienced that having children with you allows for barriers and inhibitions around expression and creativity to be dropped. This would go some way to explaining the therapist's ease when using art with individual children, rather than with whole families. Children have permission to be creative, make mistakes, and cause mayhem, so, when working with children alone, do we also have that licence? Stella discussed an experience of an interactive art piece that led to a discussion around the nature of childhood:

> *Hilary*: It's interesting because as you are talking, I'm wondering if it would be different if you had a younger child with you, would you . . .
>
> *Stella*: If I had kids, yes, I would go absolutely bananas with them.
>
> *Sunniva*: So it's something about permission.

The difference that makes a difference

"When the sun comes out"

Therapists shared a belief that words are limited and art allows a different lens to look at difficulties in a new way and see people in a different light. Therapists believed art had a place in helping to overcome communication difficulties and helped in aiding expression.

> Esme: I think it's a really good way to change the pace as well; when things get a bit stuck it gives you that opportunity . . . to do something visual, and come together on something . . . I think it can be met with relief sometimes, it can change the dynamic in the room.

Culturally, art and music were also viewed as having the potential to offer a safe place.

> Leo: Where I am trying to use it a bit is for people who have been traumatised . . . helping remind people of their culture of origin and to places where they have felt safe. I have used it to think about reaching an emotional non-verbal level, but I would like to develop that a bit more . . . use it more creatively.

In considering the "emotional non-verbal level", Leo suggested that there is a level of feeling that can be reached beyond words through music. Art was also described as very helpful for troubled adolescents who have difficulty expressing feelings verbally.

Inspired by drumming

"Fascinating rhythm"

Therapists shared experiences of using improvised rap songs and feeling confident in using rap songs, in a fun, purposely unskilled, way, to engage a young person and the family:

> Stella: I make up rap songs that he absolutely hates, and so it really works very well. So, I come up with some kind of dire rap song about his mood or his frame of mind or what he's been up to, so it kind of works because his parents get quite engaged in it and he gets quite engaged in it and corrects me every now and then.

Here the therapist's playfulness finds a vehicle through rhythm, which, in turn, connects to the young person through touching on aspects of musical culture.

The power of music

"You do something to me"

> *Elsbeth*: I know all the words and it's all in some small corridor in my brain . . . my mother would sing them . . . and I always danced . . . over the years music has become much more important to me, extremely moving and evocative.

The power of music was recognised personally and culturally by all therapists. It was, therefore, interesting that when it came to thinking about using music professionally, it was viewed as such an alien phenomenon. The power of music was described as a positive aspect of life, yet is also one so very personally connected to individuals; therefore, bringing music into professional life holds the potential to be exposing and risky. Art, on the other hand, can be experienced from a more personal distance and therefore feels safer.

Family therapy is a serious business

"Sophisticated lady"

Therapists discussed the wealth of systemic tools and options already available for them to consider, without art and music. There was a distinction made between "art therapy" and "systemic stuff", but there was also an acknowledgement that systemic work is creative and systemic tools are creative in themselves:

> *Linda*: I was sort of thinking the tools you learn on your family therapy training are quite creative, like doing a genogram or sculpt, are creative in a funny sort of way.

This acknowledgement of the creativity inherent in family therapy is important in framing the techniques in this book as just another tool to add to your creative repertoire.

CHAPTER SIX

Introduction to systemic music and art techniques

This chapter is the result of an action research project that explored and developed family therapists' experiences of using systemic art and music techniques in a Child and Adolescent Mental Health setting. The chapter presents ideas to form the basis of your own exploration into using art and music and is meant to be dipped into, rather than followed religiously. The best way to integrate the ideas into your practice is to consider your own identity as a family therapist, your experience of art and music, either personally or professionally, and explore how this might influence the way the ideas fit with your way of working.

When trying to integrate anything new into practice, it is important to be reflective about your theory of change and be willing to consider new possibilities about how change happens; this will allow you to become open to new possibilities of difference. The main advice would be to follow your instincts. To begin with, a helpful question to ask yourself in your everyday practice is "If I was doing this creatively, what would it look like?"

Family therapists who have used the techniques have reported that they are a powerful adjunct to their work with words, have "shifted things", and are particularly useful for children and young people who struggle to express themselves verbally. When trying the new techniques, it is also important to consider the wider context of your working environment. If possible, create partnerships with other clinicians to introduce the ideas and create opportunities to come back and discuss, seek out mentorship, share the new techniques with your manager and team, and include these in supervision. These ideas will be explored further in the final chapters of the book.

How to introduce new ideas in a clinical setting

When considering applying art and music in family therapy practice, it is important to consider how to introduce this different way of working to families. The following ideas are suggestions if you, too, are wondering how this might work.

It might be good to start using new techniques with families you have been working with for a while; perhaps where it is already known that conversations can get stuck or new insight/direction is needed for a family, therapist, or both. Music and art therapy are evidenced-based practice and it might be helpful to say to a family that evidence shows that interacting through music and art can give rise to new thinking, interacting, and expression, and you wonder if they might like to try some.

As many family therapists use diagrams in their practice already, it might be easier to introduce art than music; music might feel a little more foreign. It can feel a little daunting for therapist and family alike if the musical instruments are kept in a basket and then need to be unpacked in order to use them. Some therapists feel this is like a big unveiling and makes them question their skill. There are several ways to overcome this.

*   Put out a few instruments in the room before you start the session. You might find that members of the family automatically start playing them and, if this is the case, it becomes more natural to begin a discussion about using them. Bear in mind that it is often helpful to start a music activity from silence, so it might need some session management to help the family to choose instruments and then sit quietly for a brief moment before playing. However, do not let this hinder your creative spontaneity

and if a child has a good rhythm going and is really into what they are doing, you can help the family join in.

* As we know, children—and adults—are often curious and enjoy a bit of mystery. Children opening a basket of instruments and delving in can be made into a fun activity in itself. The choosing of instruments for self and for others can also give rise to conversations and shed light on family dynamics.

* Pacing and timing when using the techniques is also important. For example, a child suffering from post traumatic stress disorder (PTSD) could feel overwhelmed with the emotive power of music. In this instance, it might be more containing to introduce an art exercise to the family, at a time in the work when trust and a good therapeutic relationship have been established.

* Crisis management within sessions can be an obstacle to introducing creative ideas. In these situations, there is often a predominance of words and we can find ourselves positioned by the family to become solution focused in order to help them deal with their crisis. Often, more multi-agency work is necessary and there is a greater expectation from mental health teams to produce results. This type of situation can make it harder for therapist and family alike to step out of prescribed roles to look at the wider picture. In these cases, it might be helpful to name this process to families and gradually introduce creative ideas: for example, "Today I wondered if you might like to spend the final twenty minutes at the end of the session doing something new with me—perhaps we could use the art materials. I think it might help us to keep hold of all the voices from within the family, and might even offer us a different way of seeing things."

Supervision and training

The art and music techniques can also be used in training and supervision. Incorporating the techniques into these contexts, can provide instruction for trainees on creative methods and also be a tool that could be used in a trainee group for gaining insight into individual and group processes. As can be seen from therapist feedback during my research.

"I used that footprints exercise (see p. 70) in my supervision group . . . what we are trying to get people to do in supervision is to be clearer about their own theoretical frameworks . . . all the time people are trying to struggle with how to be creative with that, you know, so I think it would be quite fruitful to put it in more explicitly."

Both music and art were considered for training, to instruct on how to use the techniques with families and also as tool for processing in a supervisory way. The participants believed that using techniques to explore trainees' own personal/professional journeys would allow the ideas to become understood from an "inside out" perspective, therefore becoming more easily incorporated into work with families.

"If you are using them as part of your own training, then you will be thinking in a different way, as we were in the workshop actually . . . you are thinking 'oh that's interesting, that got me thinking', so you kind of understand it from the inside out, so when we are using it in the therapy sessions you've got a bit more of a sense of what the experience is going to be."

Using instruments can also be a lively and expressive way to feed back a "comment" at the end of a continuing professional development event. To do this, musical instruments can be left around the room and delegates can be invited to feed back non-verbally on their experience of the day.

CHAPTER SEVEN

Systemic music techniques

These guidelines are intended for use by family therapists with or without previous musical training to use with families with or without previous musical training. They do not constitute music therapy, but are an introduction to how the activity of live music making can be used in family therapy sessions.

It is helpful to encourage the family to start each exercise by being quiet first. Attempting to make music when talking is like trying to draw on a piece of paper when the paper already has marks on it. Comparing the quiet space to create music to a blank canvas ready to paint can be helpful in giving importance to the musical process about to happen and help the family focus on the activity at hand.

Think about seating arrangements and space. Having room to move your arms is important, as is making sure everyone can see each other. A circle arrangement, as family therapists are used to, is a good starting point.

Resources

It is good to have a selection of percussion instruments that provide various different timbres (tonal quality). A selection is listed below, but can be expanded upon. When choosing instruments, try to find a balance between Group A and Group B:

Group A instruments

Djembe, Conga, bongo, hand drums, tambour, xylophone, guiro, rhythm sticks, wood block, bass bars, wooden agogo, rain stick, ball shaker, egg shaker, maracas.

Group B instruments

Soprano or alto glockenspiel (I prefer the latter, it has greater depth), hand bells, sleigh bells, tambourine, temple bells, bass claves, chimes, cow bells, triangle.

The most popular instruments with children in my practice over the past twenty years have been: the djembes, bass bars, guiro (fish scraper), ball shaker, xylophone, glockenspiel, and hand bells.

Beginnings: warming up, making a sound, playing together, and creating music. Engagement, listening to each other, working together

To break the ice, it is important that the family feels safe and supported in making a sound. The therapist needs to take a directive approach to allow for sound to happen safely and to alleviate any fear the family might have of getting it wrong.

1. Before even trying to organise or co-ordinate any sound into a musical rhythm, it is helpful just to make some noise. This can be done by creating a "rumble" on a chosen instrument. This is done with a flat hand, palm down, beating closed fingers on the drum slowly and quietly and gradually increasing pace and volume. The therapist needs to take a lead and maybe count the family in with a "1, 2, 3, go!"

2. The therapist asks the family members to choose an instrument that interests them. The therapist then asks the family to repeat what she does and plays a simple rhythm. The same rhythm can be repeated several times until the family has got the hang of playing. At this point the therapist can change or elaborate on the rhythmic idea. Think about loud and soft possibilities, different

tempos (speeds), accelerating the rhythm to go from slow to fast. The therapist can then ask if any family member would like a turn to lead.

3.   The therapist explains that together as a group they are going to build up a rhythm starting with one person and gradually building up until the whole family and the therapist are playing together. The therapist can invite someone to start, but if there are no takers then the therapist can offer to begin. A very simple rhythm is good to start with. Ask the family to participate in the order they are sitting in the circle. It is helpful to remind the family members to listen to the rhythm for a while first and join in when they are ready, with the same rhythm or with a complementary rhythm. It is often helpful to begin this activity using drums or wooden sounds. Brighter sounds like those of glockenspiels and bells can be added later to extend the activity if it is going well. The family might wish to choose other instruments with a contrasting sound to add to the musical whole. Hand bells can be good for this.

4.   Initially, instruments can be chosen by family members for themselves. This can be extended to allow an instrument to be chosen by one member of the family as a "gift" for another member of the family. How easy is it to accept and play the gift? Why was that particular gift chosen?

This may be the first time a family has participated in an activity together for a long time. Within this simple activity, there are already opportunities for the family to experience an alternate way of being together and different ways of seeing each other. Music played in this way can often lead to laughter and open up opportunities to think about humour, joy, and being in the present. Memories of childhood may be evoked, as well as thoughts about family patterns and roles, leadership, co-operation, collaboration, and resourcefulness.

Soloists and support

Support roles (giving and accepting support), family roles,
individual voices, hearing one another

This activity relies on the family having been able to engage in creating a rhythm together in the warm up "Beginnings" exercise.

Acknowledge the family's success in playing together and invite them to form a rhythm section to support one member of the family in playing a solo.

1. Use the same instruments or change instruments from the "Beginnings" exercise. This time the family creates a simple beat together following a shared tempo (speed), and when a family member wishes to do something different or to play a solo, he or she raises a hand and starts. When they have finished, they raise a hand again to indicate that they are not just pausing, but are ready to stop; at this point, they rejoin the beat with their family, opening up the opportunity for a different member of their family to raise a hand.

2. In an extension of the above exercise, the family becomes a rhythm section on similar sounding instruments, for example, drums, and the soloist chooses a different instrument to allow the solo voice to be heard clearly. The family can play different but complementary rhythms. The therapist helps the soloist to choose an instrument, maybe suggesting an instrument with a different timbre (tonal quality) from the rhythm section, xylophones and glockenspiels can be good. If the soloist is feeling particularly confident, he or she might wish to choose a selection of instruments.

Helping the family create a rhythm section might mean having a few attempts to get a good sense of playing together (see exercise 3 under "Beginnings", above). Explain to the soloist before the music starts that they can join in as little or as much as they like and might wish to listen to the rhythm section for a while first before beginning. It can be suggested that the soloist indicates he or she has finished playing by putting down the instrument. This will allow for the soloist to have pauses in the solo without the rhythm section presuming that must be the end of the piece.

If there is a general reluctance in the family to engage in this activity, it might be that two members of the family join forces in a duet while the rhythm section supports them, rather than one person soloing. Duets can be fun to do by sharing a xylophone, piano, or using a set of hand bells.

It can take a lot of courage for a family member to put themselves in the soloist position and might be an opportunity to consider confidence, assertiveness, bravery, and different perspectives of this within the family. It might also be the case that a dominant family member takes this role and this can be explored in terms of repeating patterns and roles, what is helpful, and what change is desired or required. The family might be open to exploring how it felt to give and receive support in their various roles and how this reflects or does not reflect life at home. These conversations can lead to a repeat of the exercise with other family members having a turn at being soloist.

Conducting

Leadership, self-expression, sharing, and collaborating

Once the family has experienced playing together, an opportunity can be created for one family member to organise and conduct the music that the family plays. The family member might wish to give the music a title or theme before he or she starts conducting, or might wish to reflect on it afterwards. The conductor has the opportunity to choose the instruments played and who plays what. The conducting can happen in two ways.

1.   The conductor uses eye contact to bring in a family member. The conductor looks directly at the family member he or she wishes to join in; family members may accept the invitation or pass.
2.   Simple hand gestures can be invented to indicate volume, starting and stopping, and tempo (speed), and who should join in when. The conductor can be as directive as he or she wishes to be and might wish to have the family create a rhythm together first or play in a more *ad hoc* "sounds in space" way. The conductor can choose to play as well, or not.

Therapist reflections

Kate: I kind of liked the idea of them picking out an instrument for each other. Which would mum be? And just playing with that, how would they sound together?

Shulah: I also thought it might be nice for him to be the conductor, you know, that would empower him a bit, that we would have an instrument and he would allow us to play or not play, or us to be silent . . . he was very keen, very keen, and he had a big smile on his face when we talked about drums.

This activity can be used to consider issues such as power and control, collaboration, self-expression, leadership, self-esteem, and confidence. The way a family communicates at home through eye contact could also be possible to explore. How easy is it to have eye contact in the family? How is it understood and what do people hope to express through eye contact? It might be interesting to consider using it where boundaries are an issue, or when a child is struggling to express an emotion/feeling state through words. In this case, music might help to express those feelings non-verbally with the family's help.

Different voices

Enactment/circular questioning

The instruments themselves, with their various shapes, sizes, and sound possibilities, can be useful symbolic tools to use in eliciting verbal and musical conversations around differing perspectives and understandings within the family.

Questions to a young person in the family could include:

- What instrument would dad use?
- How would he play?
- Who else would play like that?
- How would that sound?
- Who agrees with that?
- What would the differences be?
- How did he used to play? Who would notice the difference now?
- How would you like his playing to sound?
- What would happen if mum played like that instead?
- What would you have to do with your own playing for your mum and dad to play differently?

At each point within this conversation is the opportunity to test out assumptions by playing music together.

In a similar way to verbal enactments, the family can be invited to have musical conversations with each other, swapping instruments and swapping positions to experience what other members of the family might experience. For example, a member of the family might end up playing a quiet, delicate instrument while everyone else is playing instruments with the potential for great volume. How influential can the quiet instrument be? Who can hear it? What happens when it plays? What happens if it stops playing?

The musical sculpt

Multiple perspectives, possibilities for change, internalised other voice

The use of sculpts is common within family therapy practice and can take various forms, from family members physically positioning themselves in a room, to using buttons, animals, or even objects from a handbag, on a table. Using musical instruments in a sculpt allows for the sculpt idea to gain a further dimension. Family members can be asked to choose an instrument to represent themselves, or one family member can choose instruments to represent the family. A member of the family then comes forward to place the instruments in a sculpt depicting family relationships, either in real time or in future orientated time. A discussion about the process and result of what has taken place then ensues. If the sculpting objects are instruments, the possibility of playing them remains an option and, in a similar way to enactments, musical conversations can then occur through the playing of the instruments. The therapist's role is to observe and support the process, which may elicit questions: for example, can the instruments play together if too far apart? Can they hear if too close? What can other instruments in the sculpt do to create change or contribute? Can their contribution be heard? Can all the instruments in their sculpted positions play a rhythm together like they did in the "Beginnings" activity? What would need to change to enable this? Opportunities to "play" other people can also be created: for example, dad is a drum, placed in the corner by mum, but played by the son.

As in all work in family therapy, the timing of interventions is important to bear in mind; in doing sculpts this is even more so. The very physicality of the instruments themselves can become powerful and emotive symbols: for example, if you can imagine a tiny hand chime symbolising a daughter placed under a tall conga drum symbolising a mother or father. It might be necessary to consider the instruments as silent objects in the first instance and use the sculpt as you would any other before attempting any musical conversation or activity.

Case example: Katy's story

The musical sculpt and soloists and support

Katy's family consisted of mum, step-dad, and three children: John, aged eleven, Katy, aged nine, and Dylan, aged six. Katy is being treated within CAMHS for anorexia.

I decided to try some music with Katy's family because the boys were quite boisterous in the room, interjecting regularly in conversation that seemed very adult focused while Katy would sit quietly, saying very little. All the children, including Katy, were excited to see the instruments and said they were keen to come today because I had said we would do some music. We began by choosing instruments and creating a rhythm together. The children were impressed that they could all play together and said they were all listening to each other and that does not usually happen. We did a soloist and support exercise and considered voices being heard. All the children were worried about "speaking out" and being soloists. We wondered about making lots of noise at home and no one listening and how different it feels if people are listening. The family then tentatively began grouping together to do duets. Dad asked John to play with him and they played together on the xylophone while being supported by me and the rest of the family. Later in the session, we considered how John and dad rarely have co-operative time together and are often in conflict. Dad spoke about how good it was to have the opportunity of doing something together, listening and co-operating. John was really pleased, too, and said he had forgotten what it was like to get on with dad. Katy was reluctant to play, but mum helped her do a duet. Katy was really pleased with the result and thought it sounded great. All the children said Katy's music was "cool" and sounded relaxing and smooth. Mum said how good it was that Katy had accepted her support and described feeling useful and helpful, which she had not experienced for some time.

We then used the instruments to do a sculpt. Katy led this activity, choosing instruments to represent family members. Katy placed family members at quite a distance from each other but put herself close to dad. We discussed this together. Katy then did a sculpt of how she would like it to be, everyone closer, with mum and dad outside protecting. Dad said that was how it used to be before the illness, and Katy became tearful because she could not remember it being like that. The family were then able to describe the illness as pulling people away from each other and causing tension and friction. We externalised the anorexia and considered how it had affected all relationships and how we would know if Katy had become stronger than the anorexia and could tell it to go back out the door. We shared thoughts about what would have to change to achieve Katy's sculpt. Katy liked the sculpt and wanted it to be photographed so that we would know which instruments to play next time to experience a musical version of how the family would like to be.

Improvisation

Free expression, telling a story, being heard

Improvisation is a process where the family is invited to play freely. Some children particularly enjoy the freedom that improvisation offers, while others find the lack of structure overwhelming. Improvisation in family therapy can be used in a number of ways. Below are a couple of suggestions.

1. *To chart time.* Improvisation has been used in family therapy as a way for children to be able to tell the therapist what has been happening since the last session, or reflect on a period of time. For example, a child could be invited to play a piece that represents how they felt leaving primary school, how they felt during the summer holidays, and how they feel about starting at secondary school. The journey through therapy can also be reflected on in a similar way to look at process.
2. *To tell a story.* Improvisation can be a good vehicle for children to be able to tell their stories, either through solo performance to

their parents, or by inviting the children to guide their parents in supporting them musically. This can be through the child choosing instruments for their parents to play, in a similar way to the conducting exercise. In cases where there is a lot of parental conflict and the children's voices are not heard, improvisation can be a safe way for children to begin to tell their story to their parents and express how they feel.

Therapist reflections

They were really interested in using the instruments; they really got it immediately, as did the mother, so I introduced the exercise and asked them to show us all ... in three separate performances ... what it was like when we first met, the time we met before the summer holidays started, what it was like during the holidays, and then I asked, "What is it like now that the holidays have ended and it's back to school?" It was really expressive because they are a family that use words and sometimes the daughter, the older daughter, finds it difficult to express herself and be heard and she gets very frustrated, so when she could use the instruments she could express herself beautifully and the mother could as well."

If particular themes keep coming up for a family, improvising around the theme can be useful. Future orientated questions can also be asked: for example, "How would this sound if it was resolved?" "Who needs to play what and in what way to create that?" Improvisation can be emotive and powerful and needs to be used with care. It is advised that, in families who have experienced trauma, improvisation should be facilitated by music therapy trained professionals only. However, other musical exercises in this book may be very useful.

Some thoughts on the voice

The above six activities do not specify any particular use of the voice other than talking. Depending on how comfortable the therapist is with using the voice, the voice can be brought into all the activities as another instrument through accompanying vocal sounds, such as ah, oh, uh, or through semi-sung rap or poems. For example, when doing the sculpt, further family scripts might be unveiled from which key phrases may be illuminated: for instance, "just don't ask", "I'll do it tomorrow", "everybody knows everything". These can be incorporated into aspects of the playing, reframed, expanded, or new narratives created, as part of any of the above activities.

CHAPTER EIGHT

Systemic art techniques

The following art methods to be used in family therapy do not require the therapist or family to have any previous experience in, or knowledge of, art. The techniques do not constitute art therapy, but are presented as art tools to use within usual systemic practice with families. It is important to be organised and have your equipment ready. Materials to use may include: pencils, paints, pastels, and a selection of different sizes of white and coloured paper, card, magazines, glue, sticky tape, and scissors. If you do not have a designated area at work to do art, you might wish to use pastels rather than paints. Pastels allow for vibrant immediacy but help limit any mess that might occur. Think about the space you want to use. Is your room big enough? Drawing around a table is much easier than drawing on the floor, especially for adults who might struggle. Can everybody see everybody else? Planning ahead for the possibility of using art in your session will allow the process to be more comfortable for the family and grow organically from conversations in the room.

It is important to consider your position in any activity. It is suggested that a position of observing and noticing, remaining attentive and connected, might be helpful to families. Try to avoid explaining and interpreting, instead remain curious and allow your curiosity to be shared through your formulation of questions to help the family consider their artwork. Allow for silence if it arises. While the drawings are being created, allow the family to relax into being in the present, give the family the time they need. Sitting in silence is a different position for most family therapists, but if we can bear being quiet and remain in the present we will help our families embrace it as well.

It is important to set the scene when inviting the family to use art and explain that it allows for other ways of seeing and understanding worries, as well as identifying strengths and resources.

Beginnings: doodles and squiggles (Kwiatowska, 2001; Berger, 1980)

Warming up and engaging in a shared activity

Doodles create an avenue of live art-making that frees the creator from having to worry about his or her artistic ability or experience. Doodles allow for a non-threatening, familiar introduction to art-making and are a good beginning to the introduction of using art in family therapy sessions, or as a good way to engage before a talking session.

Doodles

Each family member chooses a colour to draw with; they then take turns, one stroke each for every turn, to create a picture. Each stroke needs to set off from where the other stroke finished. The final result is one line, moving through the space on the page, ending by joining up to where the first stroke started.

Having used this activity with a child and a mother successfully in a session, this activity was given as a "doodle diary" homework task, as described by Shulah, below.

Squiggles

One member of the family draws a squiggle on a piece of paper and then passes it on to another member of the family to transform the squiggle. Once transformed, the image is given to another member of the family to adapt. The process is complete when every family member has had a turn. I have extended this activity into the "double squiggle challenge", which children seem particularly to like. One family member draws a squiggle, followed by another family member, and then a third family member is invited to create a picture from it.

Therapist reflections

> The activity of doodles and squiggles was reported as allowing the child to feel contained and connect with his parent. It also opened opportunities for the parent's own containing resources to be tapped into, as the activity allowed the mother to confirm the child's patterns in an affirming process.
>
> *Shulah:* Absolutely, yes that's what it looked like, because he would do a squiggle or a pattern and she would follow up the pattern . . . it was really quite nice, beautiful, she would follow from him . . . it was quite fulfilling, I felt it was very calm . . . he was crying for himself sort of thing and he felt uncontained . . . and it really kind of brought them together.
>
> We talked about how he is angry inside about his father really and how he bursts out because he can't really show his anger to his father or express any anger or anything, so I said to him, "What do you think about having a doodle diary?" and he said: "Hmm I'd like that" and then he was very keen and I said, "Do you have, like a pocket diary?" And he was nodding really eagerly and his mum said, "Yes you do have a diary" and I said, "Put that diary in your pocket and just when, just before you feel that angry tingle . . . remove yourself, go to the toilet and close the door, take out your doodle diary and do some doodles. How do you feel about that?" and he said, "That would be nice, I'd like that."
>
> *Hilary:* And also, because you have created the memory of what it is like to do it in a very safe place with mum, so even if he is on his own in the school loos what he's doing will have that resonance from that experience, so it's like being contained again with mum.
>
> *Shulah:* Absolutely, and funnily enough it was very containing for mum.

Footprints (Hanney, 2011)

Multiple perspectives/developing narratives

Each family member draws around their shoes on separate pieces of paper. These are then placed in the room for members of the family to step into each other's shoes. Discussions can then unfold around what it is like to be in someone else's shoes. The activity can be expanded into a sculpt and family positioning can be thought about.

Therapist reflections

This exercise appeared to strike a chord with all therapists and was seen to be very effective while also remaining simple. It is interesting that it uses the least art and the most words, therefore connecting more readily to professional experience and the therapists' comfort zone, while also being unique and different. It was applied with children and families as well as couple work. The feedback from its use with couples was that it helped a couple who were very stuck on the details of events to move out and see the wider picture. Keeping the questions general about the experience was found to be useful. The couple were surprised by the answers each gave and reported that "the change of mode created a gear shift". The getting up off seats and physically moving into each other's positions had a big impact on them, allowing conversations about process rather than detail to take place.

In thinking about absent family members there was discussion about using the footprints exercise to create "missing" parents for single parent families or when one parent holds two positions. There was also discussion around helping the voice of the absent person be heard, especially when parents are not together; either in the session itself or due to separation. This was linked with thoughts about a child's identity and using the exercise as a way of exploring the identity we inherit from parents.

Jasmine: Do you think you would have to warm the context a bit in the sense of thinking together about what those shoes might be saying, before, because it is a very powerful thing, isn't it, to step into the shoes . . .

Hilary: To give the shoes a voice first . . .

Jasmine: Exactly, exactly!

Hilary: And then you can choose, once you've heard that voice, whether it feels right to step in and how far.

Jasmine: Yes, you could tiptoe in the edge.

Hilary: Exactly that, you could literally just dip your toe in.

Jasmine: And you might never do more than that much but actually that would allow something. I think it's very interesting.

Hilary: But in order to do that, in order to put the tip of your toe there, you might need to have a whole foot in mum, a whole foot with your sibling, and once you've got your foot with mum you might just be able to tiptoe into the other shoe, because mum can contain some of that. How the rest [of the system] can support you stepping in.

Case example: Sarah, Ginny, and Jane's story

Footprints exercise

Sarah came to family therapy with two of her daughters Ginny, aged ten, and Jane, aged seven. Dad and Claire, aged five, did not attend the session. Claire has an untreatable brain tumour and severe behavioural difficulties.

This was the beginning of a second phase of family therapy work for this family following a break of six months. Ginny and Jane looked shy and reticent on entering the room, but as soon as I said, "Who fancies playing a game?" they lit up and gave me eye contact. I began with a doodle exercise, which they enjoyed and allowed us to connect again with each other and talk in a problem-free way. After this, I suggested the footprints exercise by simply saying, "Who would like to draw around their feet?" The girls and mum were very happy to draw around their feet and they also drew feet for Claire and dad who were not in the session. I started by asking them to step in their own shoes and tell me some things they like to do, and then step in each other's shoes, telling me things that each other like to do. Ginny, aged ten, was able to step in another person's shoes and think from their perspective, but seven-year-old Jane found this trickier, so each time I gave her the choice to step in her own shoes or someone else's, and she always chose to step in her own shoes. When the questions got trickier to answer, I suggested the girls might help each other, and they laughed as they each had one of their feet in dad's shoes. They spoke about dad for some time and how they missed him because he had to have quiet time when he arrived home from work. They stepped into mum's shoes, too, and spoke about her worry. When in their own shoes, they spoke about their efforts to help to make things better and how this doesn't work because they are told off for interfering.

During the exercise, I kept referring back to mum about any surprises or new knowledge. Mum was then able to step into the children's shoes while I asked her questions about what it was like to live with Claire from Ginny and Jane's perspective. The girls listened and responded about what they felt mum got right. It opened the possibility for them to speak more openly about tricky times with mum and dad and their mixed feelings towards Claire. Themes arose about being the eldest, with Ginny trying to be the other mother, and how it was all right to just be Ginny and be a child, too.

We finished the session by playing a game of gradually building up a funny person on a piece of paper (someone draws a head, folds it over, and passes it to the next person to draw the body, etc.), which mum then unrolled and everyone laughed about. I invited the family to do this exercise to build up the girls' resilience again before going back into the world of school and home life. The girls asked me to keep the feet, which they named, and requested that next time we cut them out and make a family collage. The feet became an important frame of reference for further conversations, especially when it was important to try to understand each other's perspectives.

Family portraits (adapted from Wadison, 1973)

Conversations, different ways of seeing and being seen, ways of being (the process), ways of seeing (the process/result).

Portraits can be used in several ways, as follows.

1. The family chooses one member to draw. They then draw or paint the person while the person does a self-portrait. The pictures are then discussed: what does the family member see in the picture? What did the family member drawing it hope to depict?

2. Each family member draws themselves as they think they are seen by one family member. For example, each family member has to imagine how Tom, aged fourteen, sees them and draw that image. While the family draw their pictures of themselves in Tom's eyes, Tom can be asked to draw himself as seen by the family. The pictures can then be discussed in terms of expectations and

surprises. What does Tom make of the pictures? What does he recognise? Within this exercise there is the opportunity for further drawings resulting from conversations. Tom might wish to help particular family members redraw how Tom sees them as a joint exercise.

If there are two or more siblings, the children/young people could draw themselves as they believe they are seen by the adults and the adults could draw themselves as they believe they are seen by the children.

3.   Each family member draws themselves in human or animal form. First, it could be used as a more directive follow-on from the squiggle exercise, with the family taking turns to add to a drawing depicting the family animal. Second, there is potential for a more directed and focused activity in which individual family members draw parts of the family animal separately and then paste these together to explore how this animal might fit together and work.

4.   Using good plasticine, clay or playdough, the family can make sculptures of themselves, discuss the process of doing this, and then use in a sculpt. The plasticine can be easily warmed on a radiator. Hand-made playdough is great to use, as you can make a large quantity and it is soft, pliable, and non-sticky. See recipe at the end of this chapter.

The circle on the page

Multiple meanings/negotiating solutions/a family mandala?

1.   Invite family members to sit around a large piece of paper with a circle drawn in the middle of it. Frame the activity as an opportunity to fill the page together in whatever way they wish. When the activity is completed, consider how the circle was negotiated: who draws in the circle? Who draws around the circle? What significance does the family give this? Consider both process and content.

Process: how easy was it to all draw at the same time? Did a natural leadership develop? Did the task progress as everyone would have wished it to?

Content: were there any surprises for anyone? What does each family member make of the result? If it were to be done again, would anything change? How would this change be made possible?

The word "mandala" is a Sanskrit word loosely translated as meaning "circle". The mandala represents wholeness. It has a spiritual and ritual significance in Buddhism and Hinduism. Jung (1973) saw the mandala as a representation of the unconscious self and believed that the mandala symbolised a "safe refuge of inner reconciliation and wholeness". Depending on what stage of therapy the family are at, it could be suggested to the family that they might wish to create their own mandala to symbolise individuality as well as unity.

2.   For younger children and families who think in a more concrete than abstract way, it might be more helpful to have a structured activity. Hanney (2011) suggests the dinner table idea. Place a large piece of paper in front of the family and ask them to draw a mealtime. If the family does not sit up at a table for meals, you can ask them to imagine what they think it would be like. Consider how the family arrange themselves, whether this is a given or has to be negotiated. What is the significance of mealtimes for the family? What is the meaning of food for the family?

The family drawing (Carlson, 1997; Kwiatowska, 1978; Landgarten, 1981; Linesch, 1999; Riley, 2000)

Painting the problem: an externalising activity. Multiple perspectives

1.   The family members are invited to draw the problem as a co-created picture. This is in a similar way to the childhood game of drawing a head and then folding the paper over and passing it to the next person to draw the arms before folding it over and passing to the next person to draw the body, etc. In this activity, each member of the family draws their depiction of the problem quickly, folding over their image and passing it on. When the activity is completed, the paper is unfolded and the resulting image discussed. The benefit of this exercise is that it is done quickly and contains an element of fun. It would be possible to do this activity before and after a session or at different points in

therapy, for example, the beginning, middle, and the end (Hanney, 2011).

2.   The family drawing can also be a free exercise for each member of the family individually to paint/draw/use collage to portray the problem.

What questions arise from this process? Who recognises the resulting picture as representative of the problem? What are the differences and similarities? Are there any surprises? If the family feel stuck on this task, it could be suggested that they draw the problem as a creature or partake in the more game-like activity described at 1, above.

At the end of this process, the various images created by the family, whether in exercise 1 or 2, can be made into a collage either whole or cut up.

In the world of the other

Internalised other painting/miracle question

This exercise is an adaptation of Tomm's (Tomm et al., 1998) technique of internalised other questioning. Instead of being asked to answer questions as if another member of the family, a member of the family is asked to draw as if he or she is the other.

Invite the family to consider what another family member's world looks like. For example, the therapist could say to Tom's mother, "Imagine you are Tom; now I am going to ask you to draw your world." This needs to be set in a time frame, for example, ten minutes to complete the task, especially if Tom is just going to sit and watch the process. An alternative might be that Tom draws his own world also, in parallel, or that Tom draws his mother's world as if he is her while she draws his world as if she is him.

Explore what is created. The therapist could ask Tom's mother, "What was it like to be Tom and create Tom's world? Do you think Tom will agree with what is portrayed? What would you like Tom's world to look like? Do you think Tom would want the same? Do you think a world could be co-created between you and Tom to incorporate elements, beliefs, and ideas that you both value?" Alternatively, the therapist can allow Tom to lead the questions to his mother from his own curiosity, and vice versa.

The opportunity is then created for the family and Tom to co-create the "Tom's world" picture again together under Tom's guidance, either Tom's world now or how he would like it to be.

It is possible to set this task as a piece of homework, but be aware that some families might not turn up to a following session if they feel they have not completed their homework as suggested. Therefore, homework needs to be suggested as a possibility of doing something creative without obligation.

Reflections with therapists

Below are some of the thoughts I had in conversation with family therapists.

> I was thinking as you were talking about the "in the world of the other" exercise and how that might be able to be changed a little bit, so that both parents might think about the world of the child, maybe create the world of the child in front of the child, and how the child can see their world being put on the paper by parents, and how they might be able to interact with that, or change that, or make bridges. For example, if mum or dad both saw something similar for the child, then that would connect to a bridge of understanding between the parents about what the child was going through. If one parent saw one part of it and another parent saw another part of it, how then might it go to make the whole for that child? You could do it by drawing a big circle, the circle becomes the world, or you could just do it on a plain piece of paper. You could either have the child watching that and asking questions, depending on how old they were, or maybe, as the parents are collaborating on the world of the child, the child could do their own world. What bits did mummy and daddy get right? So, theirs is the one that stays as the main one, and the parents' pictures are used to take bits from or make bridges, or join up the pictures.

Case example: Mena and Sacha's story

In the world of the other

> Mena was referred to family therapy when she was seventeen; she had a history of depression and the family was struggling to manage her

episodes of low mood, which would lead to severe self-harming and self-destructive behaviour. There was a history of depression in the family and much of Mena's childhood had been spent in the shadow of an older brother with mental health difficulties. Much of the time, to the outside world, Mena managed to put on a brave face. She went to school and had a part-time job at weekends, but her family saw a very different and very worrying other side to Mena when she was at home.

Mena's mother, Sacha, was a dynamic professional woman who worked with children. She put enormous energy, love, and commitment into Mena's life and was keen to be understanding and proactive in finding solutions. In family therapy, this was the same. However, while Sacha talked, soul-searched, and queried her approach and parenting, Mena would often be silent and, despite my greatest efforts with words, my questions did not seem to help Mena find her voice to respond fully.

I asked Mena and Sacha whether they would consider trying something different using art, and they agreed. They each sat at the end of a table with paints and a big piece of paper each. I sat between them with my chair pushed back, to be present but not to invade their space. I asked Sacha if she would paint Mena's world and I asked Mena to do the same. While they painted in silence, I sat quietly. Sacha was very industrious in her painting; she quickly filled the page with symbolic objects like a telephone, musical notes, a closed bedroom door, stairs, and books. The picture used many colours. Meanwhile, Mena painted a thick black line around the edge of the paper and repeated this until the page was filled with black, when Mena reached the middle of the paper the paint was very thick and she began painting circles, which drew you in, like a black vortex.

We put the paintings side by side and looked at them for a while. It was Sacha who spoke first. Sacha turned to Mena and said quietly that she now saw what she had not before. She validated Mena's experience and spoke of the depths of despair and hopelessness that Mena's painting showed. Sacha said that it was no wonder Mena found she could not speak. Sacha felt that she had not allowed herself to sit still enough to be truly with Mena, and that in her busy-ness to try and make things better, she had been running away from the despair, rather than being with Mena through that journey. Sacha spoke of her own busy painting and that somehow, she hadn't "got it". Mena then responded that she liked her mother's painting because the act of doing it showed how her mother would keep trying, and the painting itself was a testament to those efforts.

The art session was a one-off session during six months of family therapy. In the sessions following the art session, Mena found her voice and Sacha and Mena found a way to begin to explore their relationship and create the changes they wished to make to enable Mena to be heard and move forward.

Hopefulness exercise

Gauging levels of hopefulness

In this exercise, colour is used in a similar way to using numbers on a rating scale.

The family members are first asked to paint their feelings through colours about a situation or how they feel generally. Conversations can then follow about the meanings of different colours, and similarities or differences among family members. If the pictures result in the paper being awash with black, grey, and blue, and it feels there is little emotional "light" in the family, or for a family member, then ask if it is all right to think about hope. If consent is given to do this, put out an alternative brightly coloured paint, yellow for example, and give family members small paint brushes before asking questions along these lines: "If there was yellow in this, and it meant hopefulness, where would it be? Who feels brave enough? And how would it fit in? How would it look?" In this way, the paintings can become an outcome measure. If you were to repeat the process at different stages in the work, the following questions could be asked: "How much yellow or orange was there on the last picture?"; "Who dares to begin to hope that there can be some difference?" If it is the child who is brave with his yellow, how do the parents feel, and *vice versa*?

It can also be useful to reflect on the therapist's position. If the therapist asks permission to paint her own picture to reflect the family's paintings, and then uses yellow paint as well to express how hopeful the therapist is feeling, she can ask the family if she is being too hopeful in this situation, or unrealistic, and is that really getting on the family's nerves? Do the family feel they are being heard?

Here, the "hopeful" paintings could be used to explore the therapeutic alliance and process as well as to gauge progress and change. The therapist joining the family in this exercise allows the family to be able to comment on the therapist as part of the system and collaborate on monitoring issues such as hopefulness.

The family box

Safety, secrets, and family stories

The family box can be used to keep messages, thoughts, or art safe. The box can also be an aid to "talk about talking", reflect on what can and cannot be said, and think about issues of safety.

The family builds a box from a template. The box has a lid on it. Each side of the box has a drawing by each family member (the base and lid can be used, too, if necessary). Once the box has been constructed, it can be used at various stages in the therapy process, and the therapist has the opportunity to reflect with the family on themes. Here are some suggestions.

Does your art need to be in the box? Does it need to be folded up and put away? Who keeps the lid on the box? I was thinking about who could open it up and take something out? When are people ready to share? When is it safe to share?

This technique was created in response to a young boy spending much time in a session drawing and then folding his picture up and putting it in his pocket. If a box had been available the picture could have been kept safe but returned to, and shared, when the boy was ready.

Islands

Gaining understanding, building bridges

This is an exercise to create visual representations of islands when there is distance between a parent and child or between siblings.

Each family member is asked to paint/draw their island, depict the resources they have on their island (emotional and physical), and what makes their island unique to them. This could include thoughts, feelings, and beliefs.

Once the drawing is complete, the therapist can consider various themes with the family: who can visit the islands and how is this done? When is it all right to visit? What further resources are needed on each island? Do they recognise each other's island or are they surprised? What do they feel it is like for each other being on an island on their own? What is it like for mum when you visit in your boat?

Consider also the history of the islands: did you used to visit? Were the islands once joined?

The therapist can then reflect on the sea between the islands: What is in the sea keeping them apart? How dangerous is the ocean? Is it too dangerous to make the crossing to visit? Are there any SOS messages in bottles in the sea? Who has written them and who do they need to be found by? What would need to change in the sea for them to swim to each other? If a bridge were to be built between the islands, how could it happen? What resources would be needed? Who would need to do what?

These conversations can be left in words only, or the island pictures can be built on as these conversations progress to draw the sea and add messages in bottles, or add boats, sharks, etc.

Some thoughts about the artwork

As a therapist, it is important to address with the family what to do with the artwork once it is completed. This can involve thinking about what has become embedded in the artwork and what the artwork itself has come to mean for various family members (Figure 1). Therefore, what to do with the artwork might need negotiating, as it brings its own dimension into the family system.

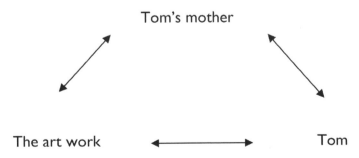

Figure 1.   The relationship of the artwork to Tom and his mother.

It is important for the family that you can offer the opportunity of looking after the artwork yourself and keeping it in a safe place. A folder for this purpose can be very useful and help create a greater feeling of safety. Photographs of the artwork can create a useful record and help a review of the work to be done with ease. If the artwork is large, photos can be taken to keep in a folder and in the client's notes.

Recipe for playdough

2 cups plain flour
1 cup salt
2 cups water
2 tablespoons cooking oil
4 teaspoons cream of tarter
Food colouring

Put all the ingredients into a saucepan and stir thoroughly. Cook over a medium heat until the dough pulls away from the sides of the pan and is "kneadable". Remove from the heat and knead very well, adding more flour if dough remains sticky. Knead until smooth, soft, and not sticky.

This dough can also be made in a microwave oven. Put all the ingredients into a large bowl and mix thoroughly. Give one-minute blasts of heat, stirring well between each one until "kneadable". Finish off as above.

CHAPTER NINE

Testing the waters: applying new methods

T he workshop component of my research was designed both to teach the music and art techniques and to give family therapists the experience of trying them themselves. The aim was that through an experiential process, the techniques could not only be taught, but also played with and personally experienced, to open thinking about how they might usefully be incorporated into practice. Therefore, I would recommend that you give yourself the opportunity to explore the methods outlined in Chapters Seven and Eight outside the family therapy room first. This could be with colleagues, family, or friends. On discussing Kolb's (1984) ideas on experiential learning, Burnham (2010) highlights Kolb's ways of *relating* to an experience, as well as ways of *transforming* experience. In Kolb's theory concerning *relating to experience*, it is not the activity, but how one senses the activity, and makes sense of the activity, that is important for learning to take place. In terms of *transforming experience*, experience needs to be reflected upon in order to become transformative and this reflection needs to lead to "active experimentation with difference in the performance of [the therapist's] practice" (p. 58) and could involve extending learners' practice beyond their comfort zone (Wilson, 2008). In the example below, Cecily appears to relate to the experience of the activity being suggested, and can envision it in practice. For this then to become transformative, she would need to reflect on the activity once completed, and experiment with the ideas further in practice, in order for new practice to be embedded.

Helping parents to focus on the child experience

"Of Thee I Sing"

When discussing high conflict families with therapists, we explored together the idea of seeing the child from the high conflict family separately from the parents. This was to help the child explore how to communicate to their parents what the child wants the parents to know or hear. The use of music to do this was viewed as a good fit.

> *Hilary*: If you were actually just to do something with the siblings or children, even if it was one child, in a way that the child could present their viewpoint, or their experience in a performance. So, you could see the child and say, "How could we, through art and through music, say that? What would we want your mum and dad to know? What would we want them to know about how you are now? Or how you want to be in the future? How could we do that in the music and what would you need me to play to help you express that through music? And what can we rehearse and get ready so that when mummy, or daddy, comes in next time, we can show them where you are coming from?"
>
> *Cecily*: I think that would fit brilliantly
>
> *Hilary*: Because I was thinking about where does a little person start, about expressing what is going on for them?

New awareness through living the experience

"Clap yo' hands"

> *Louise*: I thought it went really well, and it wasn't as awkward as I thought it might be . . . it wasn't awkward at all, um, and it fitted fine.
>
> *Cecily*: Yes, and we did it too, all four of us, he set the rhythm and we followed and he did very complicated kind of rhythms [laughter] and then

he let his mum lead and he let us lead, and there were some negotia-
tions, because at times he wanted to, when it was another person's lead-
ing time he would want to lead, but it was good, it was good.

Burnham (2010) explains that while we try linguistically to relay
our experience, our tone and body language might communicate the
experience in a different way. He believes that the less sense he has of
an emotional experience the more it becomes an "abstract conceptualisation" (Kolb, 1984). Abstract conceptualisation is the other end of
a continuum from concrete experience and is the process of trying to
make sense of the experience. Burnham believes that it is not necessarily a straightforward task to communicate these emotional experiences verbally.

> *Sunniva:* I was quite surprised [about the footprints exercise] because you
> can actually talk about it, but physically putting yourselves, it was really
> different, wow.

While some therapists questioned why you would use anything
other than words, others commented that exercises such as the internalised other art exercise were easier through art than words, therefore indicating that the techniques could allow systemic ideas to be
utilised within a broader age range.

> *Marcus:* I like internalised other but sometimes I am a bit cautious about
> using it with younger kids because I feel how are they going to get it, and
> it feels quite confusing sometimes, but it felt that that was something you
> could use quite easily [when using art techniques].

A fit with current practice

"Things are looking up"

Therapists discussed how easy it is to fall into habits and felt it was
good to be pushed into thinking differently.

> *Elsbeth:* I've been thinking a lot and talking a lot about dialogue in formal
> and in different ways, like positioning and reflecting teams, where you are
> trying to listen in different ways in order to have different conversations

and that is where I think it is really helpful, and lovely. So, you can imagine it is not just the doing of this exercise, whichever it was, that brave bit to do music, but what conversations that might lead you to have, subsequently unconnected to the music or the art, but a different way of listening, a more formal, some structure to really think about meaning and being curious, and empathy in a different way.

When words fail, the potential of non-verbal techniques to allow the therapist to truly join the young person was recognised. Rather than expect the young person to join the therapist's talking world, the therapist has the option to join the young person's world without words, to build bridges of communication through a shared "language".

Prescriptive or free?

"Let yourself go"

Each therapist will form a different relationship to the use of music and art that fits in with her construction of what is effective and what is useful. However, there was a shared belief from therapists that the simplicity and spontaneity of the exercise was crucial to a positive outcome, with good or plentiful equipment being seen as helpful but not necessary. Therapists agreed on allowing children and young people to be curious by creating opportunities for children to initiate from creative objects in a room.

> *Shulah:* They would ask, why have you got a drum in the room? And that will open up the conversation, and where to go from there.

Motivated into action

"Let's do it, let's fall in love"

> *Kay:* It is something about being with other people, you don't need loads, just one or two other people that don't think you've lost the plot.

> *Group:* Laughter.

Kay: If you work with someone else then you spur each other on and encourage each other and you make it, it's really helpful, isn't it? So, being able to do some joint working, which to be fair we do have that luxury.

Children in the driving seat

"This time the dream's on me"

Harriet: And then it is interesting, the older girl said, and I guess I had modelled this, "Who is going to choose each instrument? I guess we could take this one or that one in turns" and then she felt she would be the leader, to make those decisions and give instruments to people; actually, she was quite directive which again was an acceptable way for her to be directive, to actually be in charge of the whole exercise.

Here, the child quickly takes on the ideas modelled by Harriet and takes control, without this appearing as anarchy or threatening to adults in the room. In this way, Harriet used music and art to help the space become playful and, therefore, family hierarchy and relationships could be explored openly in the context of play.

Resonating with families

"Now it can be told"

Families were reported to be very interested in the ideas and understood the rationale for using them immediately.

Harriet: I just went straight into it because I knew this family were going to be responsive and I think words can often get in the way, or not be the right medium for this older girl. They really took to it . . . so she kind of took the floor and was dancing, really using the whole music vibe, at which the older sister got put out . . . so it was interesting then for me to think about what it means to each person in the room.

It was recognised that family culture was naturally going to influence the family's relationship to music and its use in therapy. Although certain families were viewed as "a good fit" to introduce music and art ideas to, the techniques were also seen as potentially useful to help engage very defended, private, and cautious families as well.

> *Elsbeth*: There was a family I took on . . . boys are last year primary, fiercely proud mother about any interference . . . [mum] told them not to talk to anybody because it will come back on them and these boys were quiet, not scared at all, but just quiet . . . I felt it would be very good to do things [art and music] because it would allow them to talk, or put words latterly, and might allow mum to relax a little bit because she has to be very on top of what's happening . . . trust building seems to be one of the most important things we could be doing in our session . . . so that family seemed fantastic for it.

Therapists open up to new possibilities

"Things are looking up"

Therapists believed that art and music could be incorporated alongside other systemic tools and that using creative ideas could assist the progress of therapy.

> *Nadine*: We are dedicated to family work and within that family work are the tools that you could use, so you could have art, you could have music, you could have all sorts of stuff, you could have other things . . . they [the families] could probably be out the door quicker if we could be creative.

Coupled with this for some was the realisation that there is no fun any more, which led the therapists to discuss their desire to change. The therapists believed that family therapy is a creative place that should not need defending when embracing something new.

> *Nadine*: Now you've mentioned fun I'm going to think about it more... and explaining why you are doing something, when actually it might not need explaining, being creative with a family you don't need to explain. That's what family therapy is about, whichever medium is useful to the family at that particular moment.

Giving voice to difficult feelings

"I gotta right to sing the blues"

> *Kate*: Having him pick out an instrument that kind of represented his feelings and one that he would choose for his mum, as a way of opening the conversation about feelings. How you can bang on the drum louder or softer at different times, and when he feels most angry. It was a way we could bring that into the conversation, so it was, it was really good . . . they liked the instruments, the child especially liked that it was more playful . . . I guess he does find it difficult to verbalise a lot of his feelings.

> *Jasmine*: I got her thinking about the kind of different level of noise in relation to when the symptoms were at their worse and when they were less bad and the idea was to kind of think about control and for her mum to link in with that. So, I started off with this narrative based idea and then it sort of moved more to sort of enactment . . . when they came back the next time . . . her scale of symptoms had gone from an 8 to 6 . . . it was quite a concrete experience of something being able to be diminished in the room.

In both Jasmine and Kate's examples, music is used to provide a voice for what is difficult to express through words. In using the music, the therapist has allowed herself to step into the unknown and be uncertain. What helped make the uncertainty safe is the solid engagement each therapist had with their family that allowed them to experiment with difference.

Young children like to play and they see music as playful. If we consider how music is constructed for children, it is often safe (e.g., lullabies) and fun. Therefore, when developing the techniques for this book, my position is one where, for the child, music forms a naturally safe way to communicate, as can be seen in Kate's example. However, the therapists also discussed the power of music to get in touch with feelings at a primitive level, which would make them wary of using music in specific contexts, for example with children and young people experiencing post traumatic stress disorder.

> *Esme*: I wonder if there are areas where you might need to be careful with this sort of thing? Just thinking about PTSD and the groundwork that you do before any sort of reliving or processing, and something like

that, and I remember when we did the workshop, it got in touch, you get in touch, with feelings on a kind of more primitive level.

Esme raises an important point and I would recommend thinking carefully about which activities you use if working with a child and family where trauma has been experienced. In this forum, working through improvised music is not recommended and would be appropriate for therapists trained in music therapy only. This is because music improvisation can become ungrounded and run away with itself if not held and contained through the therapist's own music-making. Music therapists have the musical skills to anchor and contain music, allowing it to resolve safely. However, there is no reason why other music or art techniques might not be useful and fruitful. For example, soloists and support, creating a family rhythm, or the circle on the page.

The nature of music

"Midnight sun"

The therapists experienced music and art as a powerful catalyst for change. They did not appear to believe music and art to be unhelpfully different from words and discovered ways to integrate verbal and non-verbal techniques together.

> *Shulah*: Yes, she played both and as we were talking she was playing it the whole time as well, or was that me [group laughter] as we were talking.

In this example, instruments become a natural extension of the communication in the room. The nature of music was seen as holding potential to engage, relax, and help a child feel secure. Communicating through music was described as allowing the child to feel less confronted by questions and therapist attention, and, in this way, helped to create a less intense and problem-focused environment:

> *Kate*: I noticed with Sam a different side to him, he was more out so it brought difficulties and problems more out with the music, he wasn't as tearful and he wasn't . . . he was much more loose and open.

In Kate and Shulah's discussion around their work with Sam and his mother, music is described as intrinsically safe and unthreatening. In this way, music allowed the family to bring more to the session than just the problem, therefore allowing the conversation with the family to be less problem saturated.

The importance of pacing

"All too soon"

The therapists experienced families being open to the use of art and music but also believed that families need time to assimilate new techniques and become playful.

> *Jasmine*: I think we will come back to the footprints because I think it was the start of something that was quite unusual for them . . . so it will take a bit of time to get into I think . . . for mum to be playful in that way . . . it was quite new for her, so I think we will build on it.

This was the first time Jasmine had used the technique, and while she recognises the need for the family to assimilate the new idea, she was also allowing herself time to assimilate. As a researcher, my focus was on how to embed ideas for the therapists; for the therapists, there was greater emphasis on how to embed the ideas for the families they work with, but we can see these as isomorphic processes occurring in unison.

Violence and resilience

"I'll be hard to handle"

> *Cecily*: We are just about to run this family, alcohol and court, team group . . . these groups are around violence . . . they have been involved in very, very violent relationships, either perpetrating the violence, or the last group we had was just women, and mainly they were . . . um . . . having their partners be very violent to them . . . the kind of things we do is to get them to think about the effect of violence, getting them to think about triggers to violence, getting them to think about how they survived, you know, resilience . . .

Hilary: I was thinking about externalisation, using art, of the violence, to allow people to step back and look at the violence, and help to answer some of those questions, just by looking at the violence itself on the paper.

Cecily: That's a really excellent idea, actually, yes, really, really.

Hilary: And then it's contained isn't it, on the paper, something you couldn't do through music.

The conversation led me to question whether art and music can be used to have conversations that do not end violently, and whether the techniques can promote thinking around resilience in a safe way. Externalising involves the objectifying and sometimes personifying of problems that are experienced as oppressive. The process allows the problem to become external to the person or relationship, allowing problems to be described in a more objective and less problem-saturated way. However, as White (1989) stipulates, when dealing with violence it is not about externalising the violence, but, rather, the attitudes and beliefs that compel the violence and maintain people in their subjugation. In stating this, I believe White is thinking about working with the perpetrators of violence and the importance of responsibility, in that separating the self from the problem does not equate to separating the self from the responsibility the person carries in the survival of the problem. So, while the therapist needs to make sure that they do not inadvertently contribute to a person's experiences of oppression, externalisation can help people retrieve lives and relationships from the problem and its influences. In Cecily's example, where she describes the female victims of violence, and states the group therapy objectives as getting the women to think about the effects of violence and resilience, externalisation through art could be a way to gain greater understanding of the women's relationship to the violence, allow for a shared group experience, and, as it is in art, also allow for the work to be contained safely.

CHAPTER TEN

New horizons:
implications for practice

W hen integrating anything new in practice, there comes a grappling with identity to assimilate the new with the old and overcome constraining factors to allow for change and the embedding of ideas.

Who are we?

"Everything I've got"

The task of therapist education can be conceptualised as helping trainees to story their professional identity, as suggested by Winslade (2002). This identity is defined as a set of values, skills, knowledge, ideas, and attitudes. The "development of a professional identity involves fostering self-descriptions consistent with the performance and skills" of therapy practice (Dulwich website). Discussions with therapists highlighted that there is a space where the definitions we give ourselves and those we receive from others, as well as how we interpret those definitions, meet. Our perceptions of creativity and how we position ourselves are two of the many issues that are played out in this space.

Sharon: People always come and seem to be in a crisis and you have to make some kind of decision about it, you don't have the time to sit down and do something like this which is reflective. How important it is to work towards that, to not always get caught up in this happened and so and so has done this.

In being a "talking therapy", words are seen to place the therapist in a certain position.

Stella: When families are in trouble, you may be in a very central position ... the musical conversations, drawings or whatever are between the different people in the room, which takes you out of it a bit, I think sometimes we can become very central.

Cecily: ... we have been trying to do some research where we have to rate to see whether we can observe family interaction, and it is very hard to do in therapy sessions because the therapist is mainly interacting ... it made us think that actually how weird that in this era, we have moved to be so central.

The therapists were keen to challenge the central position of the therapist and look at habits that have become restrictive, with a drive to introduce something new. To do this also meant rethinking their professional identity and considering their relationship to words.

To talk or not to talk?

"Where or when"

Esme: The more dominant voices in the family get to dictate what happens. If no one is talking then you can just get on with your thing and see what everyone has put [in art].

Florence: What I loved about the music was the music replacing words, the having to listen, which I wasn't very good at, but that as a metaphor I think is wonderful.

The use of music and art to help communication for those with a learning disability is well documented throughout art and music therapy literature (Bull & O'Farrell, 2012; Bunt, 1994; Oldfield, 2006;

Oldfield & Flower, 2008). In family therapy, there has also been growing consideration of creating opportunities to engage members of the
family who have a learning disability (Baum, 2007; Fidell, 2000).
Music and art in family therapy can add to this narrative, allowing for
a more equal playing field among family members and between therapist and family.

> *Florence*: I always worry about the fact that so much is spoken and your
> reliance on being articulate, um, sitting quite unhappily with that. I think
> also if you are working with someone whose cognitive function is lower,
> so I found this, particularly the music, I'm not sure how I would use it,
> but there was something I really liked about it.

The fact that music creates an opportunity for the creation of
collective sound that can be in harmony, or not, is an important difference to the use of words.

> *Leo*: The problem with talking is you often take turns, so you talk, then
> you talk, then you talk . . . when you are thinking about a family that
> might be breaking up or who are isolated . . . trying to bring people to
> do something together is, is really important.

For every member of a family to be playing together, with potential for everyone to be heard at the same time, is a uniqueness that
music brings and allows for. However, although curious about non-
verbal work, the techniques that more explicitly relied on words were
easier to embrace.

> *Vanessa*: Is there something there about knowing how to use what we
> did with the music that maybe needs a bit more practice, um, where to
> take it, the listening is really important and the kind of power issues that
> I could see.

> *Jasmine*: But we need to think more about how we talk about it in a way
> that's helpful

> *Leo*: Without making it boring or threatening, because the idea of the
> music is to access something and if you analyse it too much that is going
> to stop it.

Leo's comment correlates again with Bateson's statement (Bateson
& Bateson, 1987) as cited by Hoffman (1995) that "too much

consciousness may make impossible some desired sequence of events" (p. 44) and that music has the potential to tap into a less conscious arena. The music and art were described as stepping out of language into difference. Here, Sunniva describes, through rich musical metaphors, how music may enhance her practice.

> *Sunniva*: I think of cases where I feel stuck to help people "show" what it is, rather than talk it through. I'm thinking of one family with an adolescent and we keep hearing the same discourses all the time ... I was thinking in relation to the music, how to think of the family's different rhythms because when it becomes disjointed, if you think of their life as a melody when it becomes disjointed, when it jars, when it might meet, so I was thinking just now how to do that with them. So, at points of being stuck how to create something different, to come out of language somehow but it's the then what? So, it needs a lot of thinking, reflecting, and putting it to them in a way that they won't think "well, what is she on?", but actually think, she's got something here.

Fraenkel (2011) writes on "the hidden dimension of time and rhythm that keeps [couples] dysfunctional rhythms going" (p. 2). What Sunniva proposes is a way of looking at a family's rhythmic dances both metaphorically and practically. The idea is raised that music itself might be the very thing to both highlight and remedy disjointed family rhythms that jar.

Silence, sound, seeing, and not seeing

"The half of it dearie" blues

Family therapists reflected on new understandings of the role of silence and activity through discussing their experiences of the workshop.

> *Marcus*: It felt like a shift in mode because we didn't do so much talking but we still did something together that had meaning, a real shift to something totally different, although still trying to do something similar.
>
> *Kay*: I became acutely aware of how silent we were when we were doing the art, which also made it harder, whereas in the music even if we

weren't saying it we were making sound. There is something, I can't think of the word, there is something protective about the sound.

I believe embracing silence is one of the biggest challenges for a family therapist. We are not trained to work with silence and yet, when using art, our silence is crucial, both to model to a family that not talking is all right, and to allow the family to immerse themselves in an art experience which invites an "otherness". In order to invite silence into our work, we need to think about silence self-reflexively as therapists. What are our narratives around silence? What does silence mean to us professionally and personally? When have we learnt it is all right, when has it been deemed not all right? How do we view the silence of others and how comfortable are we in our own silence?

There were also thoughts around visibility and non-visibility. The therapists discussed that, when doing art, the evidence of the experience remains, and with this there remains the potential feelings of being judged as well as pleasure gained from the finished art product.

Marcus: There was something also about leaving a mark, the fact that those pictures are still around now and the music isn't. You are actually leaving a mark and leaving something behind, it just feels different in the music.

Hilary: In that way did the music feel safer? Because there is still something left around from the drawing?

Marcus: Yes, that is definitely part of it, but in some way I quite like one of the pictures I did, so it's nice to have that still and the music, it's organised to leave behind.

Hilary: Of course, another thing you can do with music, if your family has really got into it, is record them.

Linda: It's interesting what you say about art and the mark because I felt much more like someone could be judging what you've done, in relation to what other people had done, whereas with the music, it just seemed to blend more easily, so I don't know.

In this description, music could be seen as more similar to spoken therapy than art. Both words and music are "organised to be left behind" whereas art visibly freezes the moment. However, while words have the potential transience of music, Frosh's (2007) statement that words risk something into existence poses the idea that words are more concrete than any notion of music could be. Frosh's argument is that when words are spoken, the experience must change; this is where the risk is held, as there are many purposes that homeostasis can serve. The more abstract expression inherent in musical experience is less risky, as music voices feeling, and allows the meaning behind the expression to remain ambiguous. It is, therefore, possible that the content of words can freeze just as solidly as a picture on a page, but, unlike a painting, be less open to alternative perspectives or ideas.

Professional growth

"Spring is here"

The therapists believed that the techniques offered a renewed sense of professional self-worth.

> Harriet: I was very pleased with myself for using music as a way to rejoin them after a break.

The techniques were useful and many therapists felt free to develop their own take on the ideas, not following them too rigidly and going with the flow of the session.

> Shulah: Yes, because the handbook is so clear as well, so you can read it and go step by step if you want to ... I did think "Oh am I doing this right?" and then I thought "Who cares, it is working."

Family therapy culture and identity

"Just squeeze me (but please don't tease me)"

Family therapists spoke about how important fun is for their own vitality. It was recognised that fun is significant in the therapeutic relationship but is something that is easily lost. Interestingly, the therapists noticed a marked difference in multi-family work, which is organised to include creativity and fun from the outset.

Hilary: Thinking about everything you have said today, what do you see as the place of fun in your therapeutic work?

Group: [Silence, then lots of laughter.]

Nadine: Hysterical laughter ensued!

Group: [Laughter.]

Hilary: So what do you see as the place of fun in your therapeutic work?

Kay: It's really important because it keeps us alive. You can have a bit of a laugh with a family, or a young person, it's an important marker really, isn't it, both for the relationship and something?

Sharon: I think that's right, it is easier to have fun in a group or in multi-family therapy where you have a whole day with people you know, and you have to have some fun times in there or you'd go mad. You need space to have fun, don't you?

As Schnarch (1990) states, "humour inherently offers the characteristic of multiple simultaneous levels of meaning and impact" (p. 77); this idea, combined with Panichelli's (2013) ideas on the usefulness of humour for "joining" and "reframing", and Smith's (2011) discussion on humour and language within therapy, point to how useful humour within family therapy practice can be. Within these papers, humour is seen to switch levels of communication and increase engagement, therefore challenging any belief that fun in therapy is frivolous.

Hilary: When you came to do the art and music workshop, did it feel like it was a fun thing you were coming to do?

Kay: It felt like a guilty pleasure

Group: [Laughter.]

Hilary: Do you think that for the families that come to work with us, once we've got through the bit to make sure that they are safe, and sorted out the risk assessment and everything, that it might be a bit of a guilty pleasure for them?

Sharon: They might, father's taking time off work and not going into London, might make him feel if he's come to your session instead that you've somehow got to make it feel that it's worth it, so it's harder to go slow in those situations.

Hilary: So is it that there must be some sort of solution outcome from that? Or positive outcome that can be described in words?

Sharon: I guess it feels risky that they might feel "oh well we had fun but we can't really afford to take time off work to have fun".

Nadine: And that is society's perception of therapy with happy-clappy, you know, with making music and art. I suppose that we know it's creative and that it actually helps families connect with each other in a different way, but it's again that feeling of selling it to the client, the family, in a way that doesn't come across as you just thinking you'll try out a bit of music. Make it feel that there is a reason behind the use of those creative tools that it's not just frivolous.

Value is attributed to words over and above non-verbal possibilities and while fun and laughter was deemed important, the therapists were constrained by efforts not to feed negative perceptions of therapy. As well as questioning family therapy's identity within the team, there were concerns about whether new techniques would be accepted by families. The therapists were constrained not only by the family's expectations, but also by the social construction of art and music as something "happy-clappy", as described by Linda.

Linda: You said something about "happy-clappy" and I was wondering, do we sort of diminish what we do, or what we might do, with those techniques? If you were an art therapist, you have gone to do a particular training and you are an art therapist. Something about it being valued [laughter]. If it got out that you'd been doing some musical stuff, would people think that's not proper, that's not what you should be doing as family therapists?

Linda is keen not to diminish the value of the techniques while recognising anxiety about being seen to do the "proper" thing. Linda's dichotomy directly links with concerns around identity but also how change is facilitated, in terms of the need some therapists felt to create partnerships to strengthen their position.

Positions

"Dancing on the ceiling"

Esme: They really enjoyed it. Again, it was a family where they have a child who finds it hard to articulate things and they are very stuck in the same old patterns . . . it just opened new conversations and . . . I learnt things about them that I didn't know were important, and they learnt things about each other that they didn't know were important and mum was very surprised at some of the things that she had missed out.

Esme describes a reciprocal process of discovery and learning. For some therapists, part of this learning included taking risks.

Shulah: I think it pushed me to take risks that I wouldn't have taken before, with the musical instruments, you know. It kind of took me out of my comfort zone and I felt OK to do it . . . I have always seen myself as someone who is absolutely not creative and afterwards I thought "oh you can be quite creative sometimes with a bit of help" and it felt really good, it felt containing in a way.

The therapists discovered their position changed from a "joining the system" experience when using music, to an observer/witness position when using art.

Esme: I think to start off with they felt a bit watched, but I sort of looked around a little bit [group laughter] and sort of looked in my diary, and by the time I had done a bit of that they had become lost in it and I just added in the odd comment . . . but I think it was important for me not to be at all involved at the beginning so they could start to take owner-ship.

Shulah: I think with the art I was more of an observer of what they were doing but with the music we were both quite a part of it and we were playing music together so that made a difference, my position changed completely.

The therapist's position can be understood as a three-tier inter-active process: art encouraged a more observer/witness position, with the therapist remaining on the outside of the system, words allowed for dipping in and out of the system with questions and observations, and music created opportunities to join the system. Therefore, art can be used with words to rejoin the system and music can be used with words to step out of the system, as can be seen in Figure 2.

Family therapists reported that they feel more comfortable being less involved, and music challenges this. Therapists also observed that the techniques placed the child in a different position to the therapist

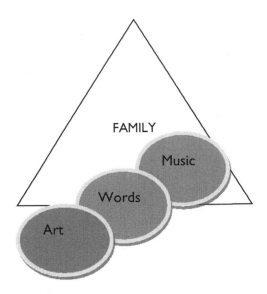

Figure 2.   Diagram of how art can be used with words to rejoin the system, and
music can be used with words to step out of the system.

than usual and allowed the therapist and family to participate on an
equal level. In this way, the music activities, especially, appeared to
break down the hierarchy between family members and therapist.

> *Rebecca*: It highlights that personal–professional divide and maybe doing
> something a bit different maybe feels a bit uncomfortable . . . I think it's
> quite good because you are asking people to come out of their comfort
> zone, it's easy to take that position, the neutral slate . . . there's more of
> a hierarchy, but when you feel less comfortable perhaps it's maybe easier
> to relate, feels less uncomfortable for the other person.

The way we position ourselves as family therapists can be seen as
another default position. Rebecca talks of the "neutral slate" and even
though I would argue that family therapists do not use this model, we
do position ourselves on the border of the system (Figure 3), which is
where words are placed, in order that we can dip in and out of the
system. Both art and music challenge this position.

It is, therefore, not just the therapist's position when using the
techniques that comes into question, but also the therapist's hier-
archical position with the family. When families take ownership, the

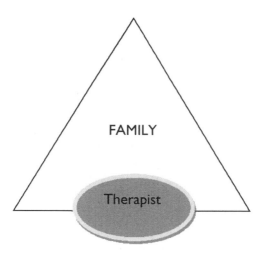

Figure 3.   How the therapist positions herself on the border of the system.

therapist needs to let go and allow the move to a more collaborative relationship.

Theories of change

"How's chances?"

Some therapists doubted their ability to integrate the art with conversation in a meaningful way and, where certain activities were particularly enjoyed, there was uncertainty about how to incorporate the ideas.

> *Marcus*: I think my anxiety or caution around those things is how can I create a conversation out of it afterwards? I think that would influence me in the decision to use it or not.
>
> *Elsbeth*: Yes, doing rather than thinking too much about it, trusting in the process. Working it out when people say to you: "I don't understand why we did that."

This indicates that a new theory of change needs to be assimilated by family therapists for the ideas to be implemented with confidence. Elsbeth believes that this theory of change involves both trusting in the process and retrospective reflecting on the process, to be able to validate the experience. From some therapists, there was an overall dilemma about how the very nature of pursuing creative activities fits in with both the team ethos and day-to-day demands of working practice.

> *Linda*: You somehow get into this clinical setting and its talk, talk, talk, and you don't have your big bag full of stuff and your sand tray because it's not all set up. So, you're wondering what other clinicians will say about sand being left on the floor, or there being lots of noise. How does it fit in really? With the day-to-day stuff?

In these descriptions, there is only concern about adults' disapproval and no mention specifically of children or adolescents responding negatively. This raises the question about how child friendly family therapy in Child and Adolescent Mental Health Services is, and who is the focus of our attention.

Only words will do

"Everything but you"

There was an assumption that crisis needs words, and a theme that music and art might be "too light" for use in crisis situations and too exposing, especially when working with very entrenched families. Here, Elsbeth and Cecily take different positions.

> *Elsbeth*: It sounds fascinating and really interesting, and at that level very useful to think of another way. These are people who have spent years hating each other ... it's how you could use, and it gets very tedious having a million conversations again about what the impact of that is on their children, but almost you would be five steps ahead if they could collaborate on an activity.

> *Cecily*: But that's why I like the music thing so much ... I think it would be such a dramatic way to show the parents the stress their child experiences when the parents may have an argument, but actually you could do it in music, it would be quite a different way to get it.

Work pressures and constraints

"I ain't got nothing but the blues"

Therapists believed that therapy culture within the NHS had changed to more evidence-based therapies and, as a result, the working lives of therapists had changed. The changing culture meant less autonomy and freedom, with the business nature of organisational change stifling confidence to be flexible in practice.

> Linda: It's all become so rigid it squashes your ability to do something a bit more . . . creativity is not really valued in that. [Group agree.]

In a climate of organisational change, ideas or projects that do not link directly into the organisational focus are not being valued. This highlights that to create change or difference the environment needs to be receptive to that change or difference and value given to the endeavour. Creativity was said to have dissipated in the pressures of adhering to the demands of organisational upheaval, and the therapists' ability to create difference felt constrained. For this very reason, joint working and thinking of the music and art techniques as an extension of what we already do is crucial.

Crisis and the default position

"I got it bad and that ain't good"

It became evident during the research that crisis in a session can lead to the therapist adopting a default position of crisis management. This was experienced as inhibiting deeper therapeutic thinking and processes.

> Florence: I found it so inspiring the session we did with you and I also want to use it . . . and I was trying to think why I haven't and why I haven't is because . . . there has been crisis and a higher level of social services input . . . so basically, since we met, my work has been crisis management, profound work in a way, has not been able to take place . . . there wasn't the space for it.
>
> Hilary: I wonder if it would be possible, only you can tell, at the beginning of the session to say, "Today I want to spend forty minutes catching up

and dealing with some of the issues we were thinking about last time, but I really want to hold on to twenty minutes at the end because I think that we seem to be crisis managing, and I think it would be really helpful to think more broadly and I would like to offer you that opportunity."

Florence: And that's a very good point ... I could have done that, my worry about her tends to dominate ... you've made me think about what it is sometimes to work with such a level of complexity.

Hilary: And I wonder sometimes if it can be a relief for the family because they come in and I guess they respond to what they feel they should be doing.

Florence saw how easy it is to become part of the complexity of the system and alerted me to the need to have the new ideas included in a supervisory context, to be able to form a part of living and breathing reflective practice.

The process of change

"Stormy weather"

Linda: I think it [the research] reinforced the sense that we are on a bit of a plateau. That you've got to a point where you know what you are doing so you can go in and do it, but actually you are not really challenging yourself or challenging what you are doing in therapy.

It became evident during the research that partnership work is important to sustain creative ideas. The therapists discussed the need for prompts and reminders to sustain enthusiasm and constructed the process of embedding change as a need to slow down, and have thinking space, a reference point, a mentor, and an environment conducive to the development of new ideas.

Linda: There is an expectation that you have to work at a frantic pace the whole time, which you can sort of do, but something new, which you would have to think about would be a bit slower.

Therapists proposed that one needs more than a desire to change for change to happen, so the question is one of how to embed ideas in a given context. Paying closer attention to external influences that might restrain and restrict creative flexibility is a crucial factor in creating a learning system or learning team to counteract dominant discourses.

It's fun!

"I got rhythm"

Family therapists expressed their enjoyment of using the techniques, and families reported they found it playful and less scary.

> Esme: The feedback from the children was that it was much less boring [laughter from group] so I thought "oh good, result then".

Families felt happy and confident to work in a different way and when the therapist did feel nervous they pushed through this.

> Shulah: So, I just said, 'Ooh, I have an idea" . . . I was a bit stuck and I thought, "Oh God, I didn't read the handbook properly and what do I do?", and then I just thought, "You know what, just do it!" I almost didn't even have a chance to explain it before the boy had picked up his pen and the mother had picked up her pen and it was beautiful . . . and actually it was very spontaneous [laughter] what we did in the end [laughter].

It is not just the embedding of ideas but the embedding of the experience of something, too, that created change (Beard & Wilson, 2006; Kolb, 1984). Through participating in the workshop, trying something new, having fun, being given permission to experiment, having expertise in the field acknowledged, and freeing curiosity and playfulness, the therapists could live the experience of using art and music. So, I would urge you to find yourself some willing and curious colleagues to explore these techniques with, experiment, and have fun.

CONCLUSION

T his book is an invitation to explore new methods of working in family therapy through creative means. I have discussed music and art in Western and non-Western cultures, to shed light on the value and meaning attributed to the arts across continents, and to create a context for the application of music and art in therapy. The concept of creativity has been explored, and creativity already inherent in our practice highlighted, to help the techniques proposed in this book form a smooth segue into practice. Music and art in family therapy, and family therapy ideas within the arts professions, have been presented to emphasise connectedness between the professions. I have considered ideas of change within family therapy tradition and the role of words and silence in constructing our experiences within therapy practice; this has allowed reflection upon the practical application of non-verbal techniques.

Unlike Decuir (1991), who states that arts therapies (music, art, and drama) are dangerous in the hands of an untrained practitioner because the arts allow emotions to be expressed at a deeper level, I believe the techniques in this book are ones that any trained therapist would be able to engage with and manage. In presenting these techniques, I am not setting out to train family therapists to be arts therapists, but to think about the possibilities, with a systemic mind frame, of using non-verbal creative media to enhance practice as an adjunct to our work with words.

I have discovered that, beyond the exciting and successful experiences of using these methods in practice, there needs to be support for sustaining positive change, and thought given to how to embed innovative ideas into existing practice. It is important to consider how we view ourselves as family therapists and reflect on our professional identity, our relationship to words, and how we position ourselves with families. Also of importance is our relationship to other disciplines and agencies. When and where is difference permissible and appropriate? Can we create a space that allows for noise and mess? What makes us need to return to a default position? And how do new developments become established in our field?

Embedding difference into established practice requires more than just a desire and enthusiasm to do so. An environment that includes a supportive team with opportunities for mentorship, supervision, consultation, and partnership work is essential if these ideas are to be sustained and developed in practice. It is also important to reflect on our belief systems and professional and personal identity in relation to music and art because "if it's not in you anyway, if it's not what you do day to day, it's sort of, kind of harder to seek the segue into it" (Stella).

Pressures of work, time to plan, lack of confidence, and uncertainty about how the techniques might be received, could make you wary of introducing something different. The Eriksonian technique of the "referent experience" might be of help (Hayley, 2013). Erikson asked clients to reflect on a time from early in their lives when they had to learn something new; it was awkward at first, but then they mastered it. Asking therapists, and reluctant clients, to reflect on something from early childhood or adulthood that at first seemed scary and impossible but, once tried and worked at, became masterable and pleasurable, might help to assuage any reluctance to trying music and art techniques (Fraenkel, 2014; Hayley, 2013).

When therapists feel under pressure or unsure they "go into that default thing that you are more comfortable with and that is a lot easier" (Nadine). Mason (1993) describes this response as understandable, but also believes that this can "contribute to a state of paralysis and lack of creativity". However, Mason does recognise that "a degree of perceived certainty is important in helping us move on through our lives in as creative a way as possible" (p. 190). For change to occur and ideas to be embedded, there needs to be enough certainty that ideas can work in practice for this difference to be negotiated. Theoretically, in our work, second-order ideas have led to rethinking our position as therapists and dissatisfaction with the notion of certainty. Mason (1993) calls for us not to assume, hypothesise, or formulate too quickly, but remain curious and in a position of "safe uncertainty" in order to be receptive to other possibilities. In this book, which is more about the practice of what we do rather than the theory of what we do, I am inviting you to enter the "safe unknown", in which new ideas can be explored.

In 2016, NHS England divided the country into forty-four areas and asked each to submit a cost-cutting "sustainability and transformation plan". The result, in what was already a climate of austerity and cuts, was the further loss or rebanding of posts, including non-replacement of vacant posts within mental health services. In conjunction, there was a dilution of family therapy identity with some family therapy posts advertised as "Mental Health Practitioner" posts and open to a variety of professionals. With this change, we need to question how family therapy identifies itself and how family therapists fit into Child and Adolescent Mental Health Service teams as a discipline. If this is in doubt, it is even more understandable that therapists might wish to stick to what they know well.

The therapist's belief system plays a significant part in allowing or inhibiting something new to be integrated into practice. For those family therapists who used the techniques and reported back, positive feedback appeared to be linked to their sense of themselves as creative, or a belief that the practice of family therapy is a creative phenomenon. If one of these beliefs was held, it appeared enough of a backbone for the techniques to be tried. However, for those with creativity as part of their cultural narrative, the techniques appeared to find a seamless segue into the work. If we look back to the literature on creativity, Rudowicz (2003) states that "people in every culture . . . are to some extent entrenched in a complicated set of human relationships and traditions, and creativity may pose a danger to these very relationships and practices". This makes me curious about how threatening music and art, or non-verbal techniques *per se*, might be to an established field based on the tradition of talking. When Keeney

(2009) sings out for "inspiration and inventiveness", it is action and words that he is referring to. Keeney believes in the importance of the client experiencing "an awakened heart" for therapy to be transformative. I believe the "awakened heart" of the therapist is of equal importance. Despite therapists' initial fears when I introduced these techniques, the techniques were received favourably by families. This highlights that our assumptions on how families wish to engage might not always be correct, and I am left to wonder whether these assumptions come from our own held beliefs or are constructed through our training.

If the received definition of creativity is "the production of ideas which are both novel and useful" (Sternberg & Lubart, 1999, p. 3), it is possible that family therapists may construct these techniques as creative and, thus, novel and useful. However, when Klausen (2010) argues against this definition, stating that it is rigid and it should be possible to engage in a creative process for the experience of the process itself, without the need for a tenable, novel, or useful result, it brings to mind how family therapists' need for something "useful" might hinder opportunities for the creative experience in itself to hold depth and value.

In the Middle Ages, it was believed that as music affected the emotions, it had a direct influence over the state of the soul. Earlier, in Ancient Greece, the musical modes expressed different emotions and music and medicine were practised as part of the same. Musical remedies were also common in the Islamic world (Storr, 1992). I believe that in side-lining music in Western society, we are also side-lining the philosophical, religious, and spiritual debates that look towards an understanding of deeper existential issues that can be argued with, but not experienced through, words. In a primarily godless, rather than god-fearing or god-loving society, the emphasis becomes on survival through concrete understanding of the world in its narrowest form: an individualistic society based on personal acquisition and status, rather than a society in which community is essential.

So, if music is linked to the soul and linked to emotions, and Western culture has side-lined music, has it also ignored and rejected emotion and spirituality as fundamental concepts of human existence? If so, what does that mean for the family therapist, who is using words, the accepted communicative norm both culturally and professionally, to then ask a family to play music or draw a picture? I believe to do so is to invite "otherness", whatever that might be culturally and personally for each individual and family member. It might also mean a step into the unknown for both therapist and family.

Therapists will use what fits with their construction of what is helpful. Therefore, a new theory of change might be needed by therapists to implement music and art techniques with confidence into family therapy. This theory of change could include an acceptance that words might not always be a catalyst for difference, that significant events do not always need to be named and spoken about to create change, and that difference does not have to be great to be different enough. The therapist's role in change can include everything on a continuum from being fully immersed in the process (a musical improvisation) to being a quiet witness (observing a family art technique).

Music and art are especially inviting to children, and can help children engage and shift from anxious positions to more open communication: "When she could use the instruments, she could express herself beautifully" (Harriet). In thinking about user-friendly family therapy practice, if a family speak a different language, we facilitate this automatically by using an interpreter, so they can be heard and understood. What if a child's or family's "language" can be most fluently spoken through non-verbal means? And what if these non-verbal means have no definitive interpretation but instead become an offering of thought, feeling, and expression played out through sound, rhythm, pattern, and colour? I believe there is something inherent in our relationship with the non-verbal that might be beyond description, and, therefore, category, and it is the challenge for family therapy to find a way to embrace this.

> Forgive me if I don't have the words. Maybe I can sing it and you'll understand. (Ella Fitzgerald)

REFERENCES

Abbey, S. E. (2012). Mindfulness and psychiatry. *Canadian Journal of Psychiatry, 57*(2): 61–62.

Allgood, N. (2005). Parents perspectives of family-based group music therapy for children with autism spectrum disorders. *Music Therapy Perspectives, 23*(2): 92–99.

Aluede, C. O. (2006). Music therapy in traditional African societies: origin, basis and application in Nigeria. *Journal of Human Ecology, 20*(1): 31–35.

Anderson, H., & Goolishan, H. (1988). Human systems as linguistic systems. *Family Process, 27*: 371–393.

Asen, E. (2002). Multi-family therapy: an overview. *Journal of Family Therapy, 24*(1): 3–16.

Austern, L. P. (2000). 'No pill's gonna cure my ill': gender, erotic melancholy and traditions of musical healing in the modern west. In: P. Gouk (Ed.), *Musical Healing In Cultural Contexts* (pp. 113–136). Surrey, UK: Ashgate.

Bailey, L. M. (1984). The use of songs in music therapy with cancer patients and their families. *Music Therapy, 4*(1): 5–17.

Ball, D., Piercy, F., & Bishof, G. (1993). Externalizing the problem through the use of cartoons: a case example. *Arts in Psychotherapy, 18*: 201–211.

Bateson, G. (1972). *Steps to an Ecology of Mind: Collected Essays in Anthropology, Psychiatry, Evolution, and Epistemology.* New York: Ballantine.

Bateson, G., & Bateson, M. C. (1987). *Angels Fear: Towards an Epistemology of the Sacred.* New York: Macmillan.

Baum, S. (2007). The use of family therapy for people with learning disabilities. *Advances in Mental Health and Learning Disabilities, 1*(2): 8–13.

Beard, C. M., & Wilson, J. P. (2006). *Experiential Learning: A Best Practice Handbook for Educators and Trainers* (2nd edn). London: Kogan Page.

Berger, J. (1972). *Ways of Seeing.* London: Penguin.

Berger, L. R. (1980). The Winnicott Squiggle Game: a vehicle for communicating with school-aged children. *Pediatrics, 66*(6): 921–924.

Bowen, M. (1978). *Family Therapy in Clinical Practice.* New York: Jason Aronson.

Bruscia, K. E. (1998). *Defining Music Therapy.* Barcelona: Gilsum NH.

Bull, S., & O'Farrell, K. (2012). *Art Therapy and Learning Disabilities "Don't Guess My Happiness".* New York: Routledge.

Bunt, L. (1994). *Music Therapy: An Art Beyond Words.* New York: Routledge.

Burnham, J. (2010). Creating reflexive relationships between practices of systemic supervision and theories of learning and education. In: C. Burck & G. Daniel (Eds.), *Mirrors and Reflections: Processes of Systemic Supervision* (pp. 49–77). London: Karnac.

Burton, R. (1632). *The Anatomy of Melancholy.* Oxford: Oxford University Press.

Carlson, T. D. (1997). Using art in narrative therapy: enhancing therapeutic possibilities. *American Journal of Family Therapy, 25*(3): 271–283.

Carnevale, F. (1999).Towards a cultural conception of the self. *Journal of Psychosocial Nursing, 37*(8): 26–31.

Cederborg, A. (1997). Young children's participation in family therapy talk. *American Journal of Family Therapy, 25*: 28–38.

Chan, D. W., & Chan, L. K. (1999). Implicit theories of creativity: teachers' perception of student characteristics in Hong Kong. *Creativity Research Journal, 12*(3): 185–195.

Cobbett, S. (2016). Context and relationships: using the systemic approach with music therapy in work with children, adolescents and their families. *British Journal of Music Therapy, 30*(2): 65–73.

Colahan, M., & Robinson, P. H. (2002). Multi-family groups in the treatment of young adults with eating disorders. *Journal of Family Therapy, 24*(1): 17–30.

Csikszentmihalyi, M. (1988). Society, culture and person: a system view of creativity. In: R. J Sternberg (Ed.), *The Nature of Creativity* (pp. 325–339). Cambridge: Cambridge University Press.

Csikszentmihalyi, M. (1990). The domain of creativity. In: M. A. Runco & R. S. Albert (Eds.), *Theories of Creativity* (pp. 190–212). Newbury Park, CA: Sage.

Dallos, R., & Draper, R. (2000). *An Introduction to Family Therapy*. Buckingham: Open University Press.

Dare, C., & Eisler, I. (2000). A multi-family group day programme for adolescents with eating disorders. *European Eating Disorders Review, 8*: 4–18.

Day, J., & Le Huray, P. (1988). *Music and Aesthetics in the Eighteenth and Early Nineteenth Centuries*. Cambridge: Cambridge University Press.

Decuir, A. (1991). Trends in music and family therapy. *The Arts in Psychotherapy, 18*: 195–199.

Department of Education (2011). *The Importance of Music: A National Plan for Music Education*. Ref: DFE-00086-2011. Available at: http://publications.education.gov.uk

Dissanayake, E. (1990). Music as a human behaviour: a hypothesis of evolutionary origin and function. Unpublished paper presented to the Human Behaviour and Evolution Society meeting, Los Angeles, August.

Edwards, B. (1979). *Drawing on the Right Side of the Brain*. New York: J. P. Tarcher & St. Martin's Press.

Edwards, J. (2011). *Music Therapy and Parent–Infant Bonding*. Oxford: Oxford University Press.

Epston, D., White, M., & Murray, K. (1992). A proposal for a re-authoring therapy: Rose's revisioning of her life and a commentary. In: S. McNamee & K. Gergan (Eds.), *Therapy as a Social Construction* (pp. 96–115). Newbury Park, CA: Sage.

Fidell, B. (2000). Exploring the use of family therapy with adults with a learning disability. *Journal of Family Therapy, 22*(3): 308–323.

Forrest, L. (2014). Your song, my song, our song: developing music therapy programs for a culturally diverse community in home-based paediatric palliative care. *Australian Journal of Music Therapy, 25*: 15–27.

Fraenkel, P. (2011). *Sync your Relationship, Save your Marriage: Four Steps to Getting Back on Track*. Palgrave: Macmillan.

Fraenkel, P. (2013). The ways of engagement: collaborative approaches to fostering resilience in multi-stressed, economically-marginalised families. Paper given at The Association of Family Therapy Conference 19th–21st September 2013 'Hope and Resilience in Hard Times: Couples, Families and Therapists' (unpublished).

Fraenkel, P. (2014). Personal communication.

Frosh, S. (2007). Disintegrating qualitative research. *Theory & Psychology*, *17*(5): 635–653.

Fryer, M., & Collins J. A. (1991). British teachers' views on creativity. *Journal of Creative Behaviour*, *25*: 75–81.

Gacheru, M., Opiyo, M., & Smutny, J. F. (1999). Children's creative thinking in Kenya. *Childhood Education*, *75*(6): 346–349.

Gardner, H. (1989). The key in the slot: creativity and a Chinese key. *Journal of Aesthetic Education*, *23*(1): 141–158.

Gil, E. (1994). *Play in Family Therapy*. New York: Guilford Press.

Glover, N. (2009). *Psychoanalytical Aesthetics: An Introduction to the British School*. London: Karnac.

Gorell Barnes, G. (1998). *Family Therapy in Changing Times*. New York: Palgrave MacMillan.

Hanney, L. (2011). Personal communication.

Hayley, J. (2013). *Jay Hayley on Milton Erikson*. New York: Routledge.

Hendricks, C. B., & Bradley, L. J. (2005). Interpersonal theory and music techniques: a case study for a family with a depressed adolescent. *Family Journal: Counselling and Therapy for Couples and Families*, *13*(4): 400–405.

Hibben, J. (1992). Music therapy in the treatment of families with young children. *Music Therapy*, *11*(1): 28–44.

Hills, J. (2002). *Rescripting Family Experiences: the Therapeutic Influence of John Byng Hall*. Chichester: Wiley.

Hills, J. (2006). West end blues: forward to the past. *Australia & New Zealand Journal of Family Therapy*, *26*(4): 228–229.

Hoffman, L. (1995). *Exchanging Voices, A Collaborative Approach to Family Therapy*. London: Karnac.

Horton, P. C. (1988). Positive emotions and the right parietal cortex. *Psychiatric Clinics of North America*, *11*(3): 461–474.

Irwin, E. C., & Malloy, E. S. (1975). Family puppet interviews. *Family Process*, *14*: 170–191.

Janzen, J. M. (2000). Theories of music in African ngoma healing. In: P. Gouk (Ed.), *Musical Healing In Cultural Contexts* (pp. 46–66). Surrey, UK: Ashgate.

Jung, C. (1973). *Mandala Symbolism: A Collection of Three Works*, R. F. C. Hull (Trans.). Princeton, NJ: Princeton University Press.

Kabat Zin, J. (1990). *Full Catastrophe Living: Using the Wisdom of your Body and Mind to Face Stress, Pain and Illness*. New York: Dell.

Kass, J. D., & Trantham, S. M. (2014). Perspectives from clinical neuroscience: mindfulness and the therapeutic use of the arts. In:

L. Rappaport (Ed.), *Mindfulness and the Arts Therapies* (pp. 288–315). London: Jessica Kingsley.

Kaufman, E., & Kaufmann, P. (1981). Multiple family therapy with drug abusers. In: A. J. Schecter (Ed.), *Drug Dependence and Alcoholism* (pp. 107–118). New York: Plenum.

Keeney, B. (2009). *The Creative Therapist*. New York: Routledge.

Kerr, C., & Hoshino, J. (2008). *Family Art Therapy. Foundations of Theory and Practice*. New York: Routledge.

Keyes, M. (1984). The family clay sculpture. *The Arts in Psychotherapy*, *11*(1): 25–28.

Klausen, S. H. (2010). The notion of creativity revisited: a philosophical perspective on creativity research. *Creativity Research Journal*, *22*(4): 347–360.

Khleefa, O. H., Erdos, G., & Ashiria, I. H. (1996). Creativity in an indigenous Afro–Arab Islamic culture: the case of Sudan. *Journal of Creative Behaviour*, *30*(4): 268–282.

Kolb, D. A. (1984). *Experiential Learning*. New Jersey: Prentice Hall.

Kozlowska, K., & Hanney, L. (1999). Family assessment and intervention using an interactive art exercise. *Australia and New Zealand Journal of Family Therapy*, *20*(2): 61–69.

Kurtz, R. (1990). *Body-Centered Psychotherapy: the Hakomi Method*. Mendocino, CA: Life Rhythms.

Kwiatkowska, H. (1978). *Family Therapy and Evaluation Through Art*. Springfield, IL: Charles C. Thomas.

Kwiatkowska, H. (2001). Family art therapy: experiments with a new technique. *American Journal of Art Therapy*, *40*: 27–39.

Landgarten, H. (1981). *Clinical Art Therapy: A Comprehensive Guide*. New York: Brunner/Mazel.

Landgarten, H. (1987). *Family Art Psychotherapy: A Clinical Guide and Casebook*. New York: Brunner/Mazel.

Langer, S. (1942). *Philosophy in a New Key: A Study in the Symbolism of Reason, Rite and Art*. Cambridge, MA: Harvard University Press

Laquer, H. P., LaBurt, H. A., & Morong, E. (1964). Multiple family therapy. *Current Psychiatric Therapies*, *4*: 150–154.

Lavie, S. (2011). Mindful-based family therapy. *The Therapist*, Sept/Oct: 1–9.

Levine, P. (2010). *How the Body Releases Trauma and Restores Goodness*. Berkeley, CA: North Atantic Books.

Levitin, D. (2006). *This is Your Brain on Music*. London: Atlantic Books.

Linesch, D. G. (1999). Art making in family therapy. In: D. Weiner (Ed.), *Beyond Talk Therapy: Using Movement and Expressive Techniques in Clinical Practice* (pp. 225–243). Washington, DC: American Psychological Association.

Liu, P. Z., Wand, Z. X., & Liu, C. C. (1997). Beijing Hua Luogeng School: a cradle for gifted children. In: J. Chan, R. Li, & J. Spinks (Eds.), *Maximizing Potential: Lengthening and Strengthening Our Stride. Proceedings of the 11th World Conference on Gifted and Talented Children*. Hong Kong: University of Hong Kong, Social Sciences Research Centre.

Lowenstein, L. (2010). *Creative Family Therapy Techniques*. Toronto: Champion Press Books.

Loye, D. (1983). The brain, the mind and the future. *Technological Forecasting and Social Change, 23*: 267–280.

Ludwig, A. M. (1992). Culture and sensitivity. *American Journal of Psychotherapy, 46*(3): 454–469.

Lund, L., Zimmerman, T., & Haddock, S. (2002). The theory, structure and techniques for the inclusion of children in family therapy: a literature review. *Journal of Marital & Family Therapy, 28*(4): 445–454.

Mace, C. (2007). Mindfulness in psychotherapy: an introduction. *Advances in Psychiatric Treatment, 13*: 147–154.

Man Keung Ho, & Settles, A. (1984). The use of popular music in family therapy. *Social Work, 29*(1): 65–67.

Manicom, H., & Boronska, T. (2003). Co-creating change within a child protection system: integrating art therapy with family therapy practice. *Journal of Family Therapy, 25*(3): 217–232.

Mason, B. (1993). Towards positions of safe uncertainty. *Journal of Systemic Consultation and Management, 4*: 189–200.

McDonnell, L. (1984). Music therapy with trauma patients and their families on a paediatric service. *Music Therapy, 4*(1): 55–63.

McGilchrist, I. (2009). *The Master and his Emissary: The Divided Brain and the Making of the Western World*. New Haven, CT: Yale University Press.

McIntyre, J. (2009). Interactive family music therapy: untangling the system. *The Australia and New Zealand Journal of Family Therapy, 30*(4): 260–268.

McLean, J., Ramsden, S., & Meyerowitz, J. (1999). Mirrors, clocks, maps & music: a South African response to family therapy supervision/training. *Contemporary Family Therapy, 21*(2): 203–214.

Mickel, E., & Mickel, C. (2002). Family therapy in transition: choice theory and music. *International Journal of Reality Therapy, 21*(2): 37–40.

Miller, E. (1994). Musical intervention in family therapy. *Music Therapy, 12*(2): 39–57.

Mumford, M. D., & Gustafson, S. B. (1988). Creativity syndrome: integration, application and innovation. *Psychological Bulletin, 103*: 27–43.

Nemesh, B. (2017a). Family based music therapy: from dissonance to harmony. *Nordic Journal of Music Therapy*, 26(2): 167–184.

Nemesh, B. (2017b). Family therapists' perspectives on implementing musical interventions in family therapy: a mixed methods study. *Journal of Family Psychotherapy*, 1–17.

Nietzsche, F. (1968). *The Will to Power*, W. Kaufmann & R. J. Hollingdale (Trans.). London: Weidenfeld & Nicholson.

Oldfield, A. (1993). Music therapy with families. In: M. Heal & T. Wigram (Eds.), *Music Therapy in Health & Education* (pp. 46–55). London: Jessica Kingsley.

Oldfield, A. (1999). Listening, the first step towards communicating through music. In: P. Milner & B. Carolyn (Eds.), *Time to Listen to Children: Personal and Professional Communication* (pp. 188–199). London: Routledge.

Oldfield, A. (2006). *Interactive Music Therapy – A Positive Approach: Music Therapy at a Child Development Centre*. London: Jessica Kingsley.

Oldfield, A., & Bunce, L. (2001). 'Mummy can play too . . .': short term music therapy with mothers and young children. *British Journal of Music Therapy*, 15(1): 27–37.

Oldfield, A., & Flower, C. (2008). *Music Therapy with Children and Their Families*. London: Jessica Kingsley.

Oldfield, A., Bell, K., & Pool, J. (2012). Three families and three music therapists: reflections on short term music therapy in child and family psychiatry. *Nordic Journal of Music Therapy*, 21(3): 250–267.

Palmer, H. (1998). The development of a music therapy approach to treating the Rett syndrome child. Unpublished paper presented to the Fourth European Conference for Music therapy. Leuven, Brussels.

Palmer, H. (2002). 'It's a family affair': systemic thinking and 'doing' in music therapy. *Proceedings of the Tenth World Conference of Music Therapy*, Oxford, UK.

Palmer, H. (2014). An action research project to explore and develop family therapists' experiences of using systemic art and music techniques in a CAMHS setting. Doctoral thesis. Tavistock/UEL.

Panichelli, C. (2013). Humour, joining and reframing in psychotherapy: resolving the auto-double-bind. *American Journal of Family Therapy*, 41: 437–451.

Papp, P. (1983). *The Process of Change*. New York: Guilford Press.

Pavlicevic, M. (1997). *Music Therapy in Context: Music, Meaning and Relationship*. London: Jessica Kingsley.

Rappaport, L. (2014). *Mindfulness and the Arts Therapies*. London: Jessica Kingsley.

Real, T. (1990). The therapeutic use of self in constructionist/systemic therapy. *Family Process, 29*: 255–272.

Riley, S. (2000). *Contemporary Art Therapy with Adolescents.* London: Jessica Kingsley.

Riley, S., & Malchiodi, C. (1994). *Integrating Approaches to Family Art Therapy.* Chicago, IL: Magnolia Street.

Rober, P. (2009). Relational drawings in couple therapy. *Family Process, 48*: 117–133.

Rubin, J. (1978). *Child Art Therapy.* New York: Wiley.

Rubin, J., & Magnussen, M. (1974). A family art evaluation. *Family Process, 13*(2): 185–220.

Rudowicz, E. (2003). Creativity and culture: a two-way interaction. *Scandinavian Journal of Education Research, 47*(3): 273–290.

Rudowicz, E., & Yue, X. D. (2000). Concepts of creativity: similarities and differences among mainland, Hong Kong, and Taiwanese Chinese. *Journal of Creative Behaviour, 34*(3): 175–192.

Ruud, E. (2010). *Music Therapy: A Perspective from the Humanities.* Barcelona: Gilsum, NH.

Schnarch, D. M. (1990). Therapeutic uses of humor in psychotherapy. *Journal of Family Psychotherapy, 1*: 75–86.

Scholtz, M., & Asen, E. (2001). Multiple family therapy with eating disordered adolescents: concepts and preliminary results. *European Eating Disorders Review, 9*: 33–42.

Shafer, M. (2008). Talking pictures in family therapy. *Australia & New Zealand Journal of Family Therapy, 29*(3): 156–168.

Shapiro, S. L., & Carlson, L. E. (2009). *The Art and Science of Mindfulness: Integrating Mindfulness into Psychology and the Helping Professions.* Washington, DC: American Psychological Association.

Slagerman, M., & Yager, J. (1989). Multiple family group treatment for eating disorders: a short term programme. *Psychiatric Medicine, 7*: 269–283.

Smith, G. (2011). Cut the crap. Language-risks and relationships in systemic therapy and supervision. *Australia and New Zealand Journal of Family Therapy, 32*: 58–69.

Sobol, B., & Schneider, K. (1996). Art as an adjunctive therapy in the treatment of children who dissociate. In: J. Spielberg (Ed.), *The Dissociative Child* (pp. 191–218). Lutherville, MD: Sidran Foundation Press.

Sobol, B., & Williams, K. (2001). Family and group art therapy. In: J. Rubin (Ed.), *Approaches to Art Therapy Theory and Techniques* (pp. 261–280). Hove: Brunner-Routledge.

Sori, C. F. (2008). "Kid's rap": using hip-hop to promote and punctuate change. In: C. F. Sori & L. L. Hecker (Eds.), *The Therapist's Notebook: Volume 3. More Homework, Handouts, and Activities for Psychotherapy* (pp. 15–28). New York: Routledge.

Sperry, R. W., Gazzaniga, M. S., & Bogan, J. E. (1969). Interhemispheric relationship; the neocortical commissures: syndromes of hemispheric disconnection. In: P. J. Vinken & G. W. Bruyn (Eds.), *Handbook of Clinical Neurology, Volume IV* (pp. 273–290). Amsterdam: New Holland.

Stein, M. I. (1953). Creativity and culture. *Journal of Psychology, 36*: 311–322.

Steinglass, P. (1998). Multi-family discussion groups for patients with chronic medical illness. *Families, Systems and Health, 16*: 55–70.

Stern, D. (1985). *The Interpersonal World of the Infant: A View from Psychoanalysis and Developmental Psychology.* New York: Basic Books.

Sternberg, R. J., & Lubart, T. I. (1999). The concept of creativity: prospects and paradigms. In: R. J. Sternberg (Ed.), *Handbook of Creativity* (pp. 3–14). Cambridge: Cambridge University Press.

Stige, B. (2002). *Culture-Centered Music Therapy.* Barcelona: Gilsum, NH.

Stobart, H. (2000). Bodies of sound and landscapes of music: a view from the Bolivian Andes. In: P. Gouk (Ed.), *Musical Healing in Cultural Contexts* (pp. 26–45). London: Ashgate.

Storr, A. (1992). *Music and the Mind.* London: HarperCollins.

Strelinck, A. H. J. (1977). Multiple family group therapy: a review of literature. *Family Process, 16*: 307–325.

Tomm, K. (1984). One perspective on the Milan systemic approach. Description of session format, interviewing style and interventions. *Journal of Marital & Family Therapy, 10*: 1253–1271.

Tomm, K., Hoyt, M., & Madigan, S. (1998). Honoring our internalized others and the ethics of caring: a conversation with Karl Tomm. In: M. Hoyt (Ed.), *The Handbook of Constructive Therapies* (pp. 198–218). San Francisco, CA: Jossey-Bass.

Tsunoda, R., de Bary, W. T., & Keene, D. (1958). *Sources of Japanese Tradition.* New York: Columbia University Press.

Ulman, E. (1975). A new use of art in psychiatric diagnosis. In: E. Ulman & P. Dachinger (Eds.), *Art Therapy* (pp. 361–386). New York: Schocken.

Wadison, H. (1973). Art techniques used in conjoint marital therapy. *American Journal of Art Therapy, 12*: 147–164.

Warwick, A. (1995). Music therapy in education service: research with autistic children and their mothers. In: T. Wigram (Ed.), *Art & Science of Music Therapy* (pp. 209–225). Oxfordshire, UK: Routledge.

White, M. (1989). The externalization of the problem and the re-authoring of lives and relationships. *Dulwich Centre News Letter* (pp. 5–28). Available at: www.dulwichcentre.com

White, M., & Epston, D. (1990). *Narrative Means to Therapeutic Ends.* New York: Norton.

Wiener, D., & Oxford, L. (2003). *Action Therapy with Families and Groups.* Washington, DC: American Psychological Association.

Williams, K., Teggelove, K., & Day, T. (2014). Contemporary cultures of service delivery to families: implications for music therapy. *Australian Journal of Music Therapy, 25*: 148–172.

Wilson, J. (2008). *The Performance of Practice.* London: Karnac.

Winnicott, D. W. (1971). *Playing and Reality.* Oxford: Penguin.

Winslade, J. (2002). Storying professional identity: from an interview with John Winslade. *International Journal of Narrative and Community Work,* 4: 33. Available at: www.dulwichcentre.com.au

Wonder, J., & Blake, J. (1992). Creativity East and West: intuition vs. logic? *Journal of Creative Behavior, 26*(3): 172–185.

Wood, J., Sandford, S., & Bailey, E. (2016). The whole is greater. Developing music therapy services in the National Health Service: a case study revisited. *British Journal of Music Therapy, 30*(1): 36–46.

Woodcock, J. (2003). Comment on: Manicom, H., & Boronska, T. (2003). Co-creating change within a child protection system: integrating art therapy with family therapy practice. *Journal of Family Therapy, 25*(3): 233–235.

Woodward, A. (2004). Music therapy for autistic children and their families: a creative spectrum. *British Journal of Music Therapy, 18*(1): 8–14.

Zdenek, M. (1988). Right brain techniques: a catalyst for creative thinking and internal focusing. *Psychiatric Clinics of North America, 1*(3): 427–441.

Zimmerman, T. S., & Shepherd, S. D. (1993). Externalizing the problem of bulimia: conversation, drawing, and letter writing in group therapy. *Journal of Systemic Therapies, 12*: 22–31.

INDEX

Abbey, S. E., 41
Allgood, N., 26
Aluede, C. O., 28
Alvin, J., 27
Anderson, H., 7
anger, 2–5, 31, 71, 91
anorexia, 35, 64–65
anxiety, 46–48, 102, 105, 115
Aristotle, 16
Asen, E., 35
Ashiria, I. H., 18–19
Austern, L. P., 16

Bailey, E., 28
Bailey, L. M., 24
Ball, D., 34
Bateson, G., 9, 11, 43, 97
Bateson, M. C., 97
Baum, S., 97
Beard, C. M., 109
behaviour(al), xvii, 18, 30, 39
    change, xvi

dialectical, 41
difficulties, 27
    severe, 73
interactional, xv
patterns, 32
self-destructive, 79
Bell, K., 28
Berger, L. R., 33, 70
Bishop, G., 34
Blake, J., 19
Bogan, J. E., 38
Boronska, T., 34
Bowen, M., 30
Bradley, L. J., xxiv, 29
brain (*passim*)
    activity, 40
    function, xxv
    human, 38
    left, 37–38, 40
    limbic, 42
    mechanisms, 38
    right, 37–40

stem, xvii
tumour, 73
whole, xvii
witnessing, 42
Bruscia, K. E., 25, 27
Bull, S., 96
Bunce, L., 25
Bunt, L., 96
Burnham, J., 85, 87
Burton, R., 17

Carlson, L. E., 41
Carlson, T. D., xxiv, 31, 34, 76
Carnevale, F., 10
case studies
    Alice, 1–6, 8–11
    Katy, 64–65
    Mena and *Sacha*, 78–80
    Sam, 92–93
    Sarah, *Ginny*, and *Jane*, 73–74
    Tom, 74–75, 77–78, 82
Cederborg, A., 32
Chan, D. W., 19
Chan, L. K., 19
Child and Adolescent Mental Health
    Services (CAMHS), xiii, 49, 53,
    64, 106, 113
Cobbett, S., xxiv, 27
Colahan, M., xxiv, 35
Collins, J. A., 20
conscious(ness), 7, 9–11, 43, 98
    see also: unconscious
    aspects, 33
    effort, 9
    experience, 44
    process, 43
    self-, 46
crisis, 55, 96, 106–107
    existential, 43
    families in, 27, 37
    management, 55, 107–108
    situations, 106
Csikszentmihalyi, M., 18
culture, xiv, xvi–xvii, xxv, 8, 20, 113
    aboriginal, 13–14

African, 15, 18
Arab, 19
Bolivian, 15
changing, 107
of childhood, 34
contemporary, 16
continuation of, 19
Eastern, 18
family, 27, 89
individual, 19
musical, 52
organisational, 49
of origin, 51
role of, 40
studies of, 18
team, 49
therapy, 100, 107
Western, 14, 16–17, 111, 114

Dallos, R., 7
Dare, C., 35
Day, J., xix
Day, T., 26
de Bary, W. T., 14
Decuir, A., 24, 111
Department of Education (DoE),
    16
development(al), 8, 10, 18, 20, 23, 33,
    40–41, 95, 108, 112
    age, 26
    of creativity, 20
    exciting, 27
    pathway, 8
    professional, 56
    of self, 8
    stage, 9
disorder
    eating, 35
    paediatric, 24
    post traumatic stress, 55, 91
Dissanayake, E., 38
Draper, R., 7

Edwards, B., 38
Edwards, J., 25

Eisler, I., 35
Epston, D., 31, 34
Erdos, G., 18–19

family art evaluation approach
    (FAE), 30
Fidell, B., 97
Fitzgerald, E., 45, 115
Flower, C., 25, 97
Forrest, L., 27–28
Fraenkel, P., xxv, 29, 98, 112
Frosh, S., 43, 100
Fryer, M., 20

Gacheru, M., 19
Gardner, H., 19
Gazzaniga, M. S., 38
Gil, E., 29
Glover, N., 17
Goolishan, H., 7
Gorell Barnes, G., 8
Gustafson, S. B., 17

Haddock, S., 32
Hakomi method, 42
Hanney, L., 32, 71, 76–77
Hayley, J., 112
Hendricks, C. B., xxiv, 29
Hibben, J., 24–25
Hills, J., 10, 28
Hoffman, L., 8–10, 43, 97
Horton, P. C., 38
Hoshino, J., xxiv, 33
Hoyt, M., 77
humour, xvii, 19, 59, 101

identity, 1, 48, 53, 72, 95, 100, 102
    child's, 72
    ethnic, 29
    family therapy, 102, 113
    new, 10
    personal, 112
    professional, xxiii, 8, 47–48, 95–96,
        112
    theoretical, 8

interaction, xv, xix, 26, 33, 41 see also:
        behaviour
    client–therapist, 25
    family, 96
    healing, xvii
    here-and-now, xvi
    mother–baby, 25–26
    musical, 7
    positive, 27
    processes, xvi
    rehearsals of, 34
    verbal, xiv, 23
    web of, 9
intervention, xvi, xxv, 32, 64
    art, 33
    effective, 25
    family group, 26
    musical, 25, 29, 41
    practical, 33
    therapeutic, 17, 34, 41
Irwin, E. C., 29

Janzen, J. M., 15
Jung, C., 76

Kabat Zin, J., 41
Kass, J. D., 41
Kaufman, E., 35
Kaufmann, P., 35
Keene, D., 14
Keeney, B., 20–21, 113–114
Kerr, C., xxiv, 33
Keyes, M., 31
Khleefa, O. H., 18–19
Klausen, S. H., 17, 114
Kolb, D. A., 85, 87, 109
Kozlowska, K., 32
Kurtz, R., 42
Kwiatkowska, H., xxiv, 30–32

LaBurt, H. A., 34
Landgarten, H., 31–32, 34, 76
Langer, S., 39
Laquer, H. P., 34
Lavie, S., 42

Le Huray, P., xix
Levine, P., 42
Levitin, D., xvii
Linesch, D. G., 23, 31–32, 76
Liu, C. C., 19
Liu, P. Z., 19
Lowenstein, L., xxiv, 21, 29, 35
Loye, D., 38
Lubart, T. I., 17, 114
Ludwig, A. M., 18–19
Lund, L., 32

Mace, C., 41
Madigan, S., 77
Magnussen, M., 31
Malchiodi, C., 31–32
Malloy, E. S., 29
Man Keung Ho, xxiv, 29
Manicom, H., 34
Mason, B., 9, 112–113
McDonnell, L., 24
McGilchrist, I., 14, 37, 39–40
McIntyre, J., viii–xxiv, 26
McLean, J., 29
melancholia, 16–17
Meyerowitz, J., 29
Mickel, C., 29
Mickel, E., 29
Miller, E., 25, 39
mindful(ness), 41
    art, 42
    based
        cognitive therapy, 41
        family therapy, 42
        stress reduction, 41
        techniques, 42
        therapeutic interventions, 41
    music, 42
    practices, 41
    spaces, xxv
    state, 42
Morong, E., 34
Mumford, M. D., 17
Murray, K., 34

National Health Service (NHS), 28,
    49, 107, 113
National Institute for Mental Health,
    Maryland, 30
National Plan for Music Education,
    16
Nemesh, B., xxiv, 26–27, 29–30
Nietzsche, F., 43

object, xvii, xxiii, 8
    creative, 88
    ordinary, 17
    sculpting, 63
    silent, 64
    symbolic, 79
objective(ly), 19, 94 see also: systemic
    clinical, 24
    government policy, 26
    therapeutic, 24
    therapy
        family, 25
        group, 94
O'Farrell, K., 96
Oldfield, A., 25–26, 28, 96–97
Opiyo, M., 19
Oxford, L., 21

Palmer, H., xxiv, 25, 29
Panichelli, C., 101
Papp, P., xvi, 9
Pavlicevic, M., 27
Piercy, F., 34
Pool, J., 28

Ramsden, S., 29
Rappaport, L., 41
Real, T., 8
re-making, 10
re-scripting, 10
Riley, S., xxiv, 31–32, 76
Rober, P., xxiv, 34
Robinson, P. H., xxiv, 35
Rubin, J., 31
Rudowicz, E., 18–19, 113
Ruud, E., 27

safe uncertainty, 9, 113
Sandford, S., 28
Satir, V., xv–xvi, 27, 42
Schnarch, D. M., 101
Schneider, K., 31
Scholtz, M., 35
sculpt(ing), 3, 8, 52, 63–65, 67, 72, 75
    family, xvi
    musical, 63–64
self, xxiv, 8–9, 30, 34, 55, 94 *see also*:
        behaviour, conscious,
        development, unconscious
    -cure, 16
    -description, 95
    -disclosure, 42
    -esteem, 62
    -expression, xvii, 19, 23, 25, 61–62
    -harm, 1, 79
    known, xx
    observing, 42
    -portraits, 31, 33, 74
    professional, 21
    -reflexively, 99
    unknown, xx
    -worth, 100
Settles, A., xxiv, 29
Shafer, M., xxiv, 32
Shapiro, S. L., 41
Shepherd, S. D., 34
Slagerman, M., 35
Smith, G., 101
Smutny, J. F., 19
Sobol, B., 30–31
Sori, C. F., 29
Sperry, R. W., 38
Stein, M. I., 17
Steinglass, P., 35
Stern, D., 8
Sternberg, R. J., 17, 114
Stige, B., 27
Stobart, H., 15
Storr, A., 13, 38, 114
Strelinck, A. H. J., 34
symbol(-ism), 2, 4, 13, 38, 62, 64, 76,
    79

systemic, 8, 10, 47, 52
    approaches, 27, 33
    art, 53
    consideration, 26
    ideas, xx, xxiv, 87
    methods, 25
    mind frame, 112
    music, 53
    objectives, 25
    practice, 1, 69
    psychotherapy, xxiv, 1, 20
    techniques, xxiii
    terms, 8
    thinking, 23, 27
    tools, 52, 90
    work, 52

Teggelove, K., 26
Tomm, K., 11, 77
Trantham, S. M., 41
Tsunoda, R., 14

Ulman, E., 30
unconscious(ness), 9 *see also*:
        conscious
    experience, 44
    family life, 30
    process, 43
    self, 76

violence, 93–94

Wand, Z. X., 19
Warwick, A., 25
Whitaker, C., 42
White, M., 31, 34, 94
Wiener, D., 21
Williams, K., 26, 30
Wilson, J. P., 85, 109
Winnicott, D. W., 17
Winslade, J., 95
Wonder, J., 19
Wood, J., 28
Woodcock, J., 33
Woodward, A., 25

world (*passim*)
    art therapy, 31
    emotional, 42
    Islamic, 114
    material, 14
    mother's, 77
    outside, 79
    real, 29
    talking, 88
    wider, 37

Yager, J., 35
Yue, X. D., 19

Zdenek, M., 38
Zimmerman, T. S., 32, 34